# Dollars & Sense

*This work is dedicated to Montana's innovative child care providers who showed us that child care businesses can be profitable, and how.*

# Dollars & Sense

## Planning for Profit
## in Your Child Care Business

## Janet Bush

*Montana Child Care Resource & Referral Network*

Africa • Australia • Canada • Denmark • Japan • Mexico • New Zealand • Philippines
Puerto Rico • Singapore • Spain • United Kingdom • United States

## NOTICE TO THE READER

**Delmar Staff:**

Business Unit Director: Susan L. Simpfenderfer
Executive Editor: Marlene McHugh Pratt
Acquisitions Editor: Erin O'Connor Traylor
Executive Production Manager: Wendy A. Troeger
Production Editor: Sandra Woods

Technology Project Manager: Kimberlie Schryer
Executive Marketing Manager: Donna J. Lewis
Channel Manager: Nigar Hale
Editorial Assistant: Alexis Ferraro
Cover Design: Linda DeMasi

COPYRIGHT © 2001

Delmar is a division of Thomson Learning. The Thomson Learning logo is a registered trademark used herein under license.

Printed in the United States of America

1 2 3 4 5 6 7 8 9 10 XXX 05 04 03 02 01 00

For more information, contact Delmar, 3 Columbia Circle, PO Box 15015, Albany, NY 12212-0515; or find us on the World Wide Web at http://www.delmar.com or http://www.EarlyChildEd.Delmar.com

**Asia**
Thomson Learning
60 Albert Street, #15-01
Albert Complex
Singapore 189969

**Japan:**
Thomson Learning
Palaceside Building 5F
1-1-1 Hitotsubashi, Chiyoda-ku
Tokyo 100 0003 Japan

**Australia/New Zealand:**
Nelson/Thomson Learning
102 Dodds Street
South Melbourne, Victoria 3205
Australia

UK/Europe/Middle East
Thomson Learning
Berkshire House
168-173 High Holborn
London
WC1V 7AA United Kingdom

Thomas Nelson & Sons LTD
Nelson House
Mayfield Road
Walton-on-Thames
KT 12 5PL United Kingdom

**Latin America:**
Thomson Learning
Seneca, 53
Colonia Polanco
11560 Mexico D.F. Mexico

**South Africa:**
Thomson Learning
Zonnebloem Building
Constantia Square
526 Sixteenth Road
P.O. Box 2459
Halfway House, 1685
South Africa

**Canada:**
Nelson/Thomson Learning
1120 Birchmount Road
Scarborough, Ontario
Canada M1K 5G4

**Spain:**
Thomson Learning
Calle Magallanes, 25
28015-MADRID
ESPANA

**International Headquarters:**
Thomson Learning
International Division
290 Harbor Drive, 2nd Floor
Stamford, CT 06902-7477

Library of Congress Cataloging-in-Publication Data

Bush, Janet.
    Dollars & sense : planning for profit in your child care business / Janet Bush.—1st ed.
        p.    cm.
    Includes bibliographical references and index.
    ISBN 0-7668-2236-2
    1. Day care centers—Administration.    I. Title: Dollars and sense.    II. Title.

    HQ778.5 .B87 2001
    362.71'2'0973—dc21

                                    00-034073

# Contents

# Preface

If you are a child care provider, business may not be in your background! So how are you going to keep your small child care business afloat and earn a livable wage? *Dollars & Sense: Planning for Profit in Your Child Care Business* can teach you the simple skills you need to improve your profitability and your relationships with customers.

Providers across the nation express concerns about poverty-level incomes. Low wages contribute directly to the rapid rate at which child care providers close their businesses and leave the field of early childhood services. Most new providers enter the field without projecting a budget, and even veteran providers have trouble calculating last year's net income.

When the Montana Child Care Resource & Referral Network began to develop this business training curriculum for use by providers in frontier, rural, and urban areas across our state, we didn't know how to manage a small business either. We tapped the expertise of the Montana Community Development Corporation, a small business development center. And they led us to local child care industry leaders—providers who had demonstrated quality care, longevity, and experience in the field and had an admirable profitability.

We noticed immediately that these innovators had developed firm policies to limit loss of income in times of market or customer inconsistency. They perceived themselves as professionals deserving the same courtesies and compensations earned by doctors, accountants, and retailers. Finally, they were advocates for their profession, and they often mentored new providers informally.

**Note!**

This training is not simply a collection of new provider skills. It teaches a new attitude about the self-determined professionalism and compensation of child care providers.

Many providers enter the child care field because they enjoy working with children, never anticipating the degree to which they will be required to work closely (and often stressfully) with parents. Our industry innovators reported remarkably low stress in their relationships with parents. They demonstrated excellent spoken and written communication skills, and they were very clear in describing the boundaries of their professional relationships with customers. With this in mind, we built a communication component into our business training. After all, what good does it do for a provider to draft state-of-the-art contracts and policies if she does not have the confidence or communication skills to enforce them?

*Dollars & Sense* supports providers in transforming their role from "babysitters" to "early childhood professionals." We suffer from an inconsistency in our cultural value system that tells us, "Nurturing and money don't mix." In other words, if you love children, you should not be concerned about money, and if you are concerned about money, then you do not really love children. Our child care system has operated on the inherent assumption that, regardless of how little they are paid, providers will still offer high-quality care just because they love children.

We are ready to challenge these notions! As women in other human service professions such as nursing and elementary education have proven, nurturers *can* demand livable wages for their work. Child care providers need training and support to ask for adequate compensation and reasonable working conditions for their services.

## ACKNOWLEDGMENTS

This work would not have been possible without the support and expertise of Marilyn White of the Montana Community Development Corporation and Kathy Miller Green of University of Montana Rural Institute on Disabilities Child Care Plus+.

The author and Delmar would like to express their gratitude to the following professionals who offered numerous, valuable suggestions:

Maria Green
Instructor, Child Development
Moorpark Community College
Monopark, CA

Nina Mazloff
Becker College
Leicester, MA

Kathy Head
Lorain County Community
   College
Elyria, OH   44035

Gretchen Kolb
Director, Rocking Unicorn
   Nursery School
Harwich, MA

*Dollars & Sense: Planning for Profit in Your Child Care Business* teaches basic skills to people who do not have experience in small business management. It highlights the best practices that are common to all small businesses and the profitability strategies unique to the child care industry.

Over this course of study, you will develop a professional business plan that includes a contract, break-even analysis, record-keeping system, cash flow plan, income statement, balance sheet, and marketing calendar. It is essential that you complete the exercises and homework assignments and that you study the examples included in the six Business Lessons. This is how you will learn to apply new business techniques to your individual child care circumstances. Examples of various business documents are given in Appendix A. They were developed by Western Montana providers to meet unique needs. They are not meant to be copied, but to be studied and adapted for your own use. Appendix B has reproducible forms for your convenience.

*Dollars & Sense* also includes six Communication Lessons that build understanding of the basic principles of assertive communication and conflict resolution. Many child care-specific examples are provided. Act out the role-play exercises quietly in your head or actively with a friend, in order to experiment with new communication skills. *Dollars & Sense* by no means exhausts the broad topic of provider/parent partnerships, and additional resources are listed in Appendix C.

Although *Dollars & Sense* has been edited to serve as a self-study tool, two heads are still better than one! Readers are encouraged to seek support, feedback, and expertise from fellow providers, business owners, early childhood trainers, and small business development centers.

For early childhood trainers wishing to offer *Dollars & Sense* in a group learning environment, a Trainer's Manual and auxiliary training materials are available from the Montana Child Care Resource & Referral Network. The course has been approved for university credits and Continuing Education Units (CEUs) in several states. For more information, contact the Montana CCR&R Network at (406) 549-1028.

# Setting Your Professional Goals

## GOALS FOR YOUR STUDY OF *DOLLARS & SENSE*

Unlike most child care training, which focuses on the personal relationship between provider and child, this course focuses on the business relationship between provider and parent. Many of the most common disputes between providers and parents are eliminated when providers improve communication and business skills. The following goals will help you guide and evaluate your training. Sign this contract to signify your commitment to work toward these goals:

> **Note!**
>
> This training is not simply a collection of new provider skills. It is a new attitude about the professionalism of child care providers.

✔ I will consider myself a professional, and I will expect appropriate work conditions and compensation.

✔ I will use basic practices common to small businesses (written contract and policies, record-keeping system, cash flow plan, competitive pricing, and marketing).

✔ I will improve my communication with parents about my professional role as caregiver, my philosophy of quality child care, and my business policies.

✔ I will increase my understanding of parent concerns, enforce my policies assertively, and treat parents with compassion and professionalism.

"Hi! I'm Felicia. I own a home child care business. I'm going to be your mentor as you study this course. My goals as a provider are to make a living wage at my job, to feel financially secure, and to offer stable service to my families."

✔ Provider Personal Goal #1

✐ _____

✐ _____

✐ _____

✔ Provider Personal Goal #2

✐ _____

✐ _____

✐ _____

"Hello! I'm Chris. I'm Felicia's business partner. Together we care for 12 children. My goal is to have clear relationships with parents. From the beginning of their contract with us, parents understand what we expect of them."

# A Child Care Provider Bill of Rights

If you are a child care provider, you are probably a nurturing person by nature. Even though you have no problem protecting the feelings and rights of other people, you may not be as good at protecting your own rights!

Sometimes we have to remind ourselves that child care providers are workers and business owners. Caring for children in your home is a business, and being a child care provider is a job. Every worker has basic rights. Unfortunately, compared to unionized workers like school teachers and nurses, the child care profession is young and relatively unorganized.

**Note!**

Child care providers are professionals, and they are entitled to good work conditions and worker status.

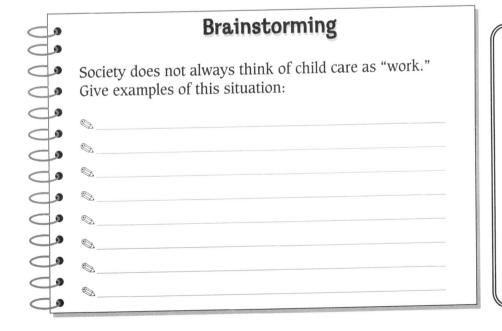

### Brainstorming

Society does not always think of child care as "work." Give examples of this situation:

"I have learned to ask myself, 'What kind of professional interactions do I want and deserve when I work with parents and other members of my community?'"

"Right on, ladies and gentlemen. Let the revolution begin!"

# Brainstorming
## A Child Care Provider/Business Owner Has The Right:

Make a list of child care provider rights. Keep in mind the kinds of professional rights that other workers enjoy. Also, think of the situations that you perceive as unprofessional or devaluing. Here are some examples to start you off.

✔ to reasonably limit the hours that she works each day
✔ to be paid on time
✔ to have a private life outside of work
✔ to change business policies
✔ to set personal boundaries regarding parents and their problems

_____
_____
_____
_____
_____

"Good job! Now keep these issues in mind as we discuss contracts and policies."

# Brainstorming
## No one Has The Right To Do This To A Child Care Provider/Business Owner:

_____
_____
_____
_____
_____
_____
_____
_____

"That's right. Now you can begin to learn strategies to keep your business from steadily losing money."

# 2

# Contracts and Policies

## CONTRACTS AND POLICIES

One of your first goals as a professional child care provider is to be financially secure so that you can offer a stable service to the families you serve. Another goal is to develop trusting partnerships with parents. Child care business policies should reflect the individual needs, strengths, goals, and day-to-day operations of your child care program.

In this and following chapters, you will learn about business "best practices" that have been developed by innovative child care providers. Working from these, you can assemble the components of policies and practices that support your goals as a child care professional. See Appendix A for sample contracts and policy statements.

> **Note!**
>
> Contracts should clarify provider/parent expectations. Business policies should maximize profitability.

### Contracts

These business topics should be addressed in your legal contract with parents:

- ✔ names of adults with whom you will work (that is, adults who will drop off or pick up children and adults who will pay)
- ✔ addresses, phone numbers, social security numbers, and employers of payers
- ✔ addresses and phone numbers of adults who will pick up/drop off children (some providers request a photocopy of a driver's licenses or other photo ID)

- ✔ days and hours reserved for child's care
- ✔ rate of pay, third-party payment arrangements, payment schedule
- ✔ scheduled and unscheduled child absences
- ✔ penalty fees (overtime fees, late pickup fees, late payment fees)
- ✔ supplemental fees (activities fee, transportation fee, insurance fee, registration fee)
- ✔ termination of contract procedures
- ✔ substitute care arrangements
- ✔ sick child exclusion policies
- ✔ medical and emergency release forms

## Policies

Your written policy statement describes these details of your business:

- ✔ description of program philosophy
- ✔ adult-to-child ratios
- ✔ behavior guidance policy statement
- ✔ basic daily schedule
- ✔ supplies that parents will bring
- ✔ your specific expectations of parents (for example, "Children will arrive fed and fully dressed.")
- ✔ plans or procedures for parent/provider meetings or conferences
- ✔ regularly scheduled special events (for example, Library Story Hour)
- ✔ transportation of children to school and/or classes
- ✔ special activities and costs (for example, swimming class, dance class)
- ✔ emergency procedures

## LIST ADULTS WITH WHOM YOU AGREE TO WORK

Require the signature of parents and/or guardians who share primary custody of the child and/or responsibility for payment. Who, besides biological parents, might need to sign your contract?

✎ _____

✎ _____

If other adults will be authorized to drop off or pick up the child, list their names on the contract. If the custodial caregiver changes as the result of a divorce or other legal proceeding, revise your contract to document that change.

## LIST DAYS AND HOURS OF RESERVED CARE

Charge parents for all of the hours of care that they reserve, even if they do not use them. Parents purchase a *reservation* or *time slot* in your child care program, which you agree to hold for them and will not market to another family. If they don't show up to use their reserved care, you have lost the opportunity to market and gain payment for that slot. That is why innovative providers expect parents to pay for reserved hours, whether the child is present or not. Compare this policy with other businesses that reserve a service for you, for example, airlines or time-share condominiums. How does this innovation protect child care providers from losing income?

✎ _____

Limit the hours during which service will be available. It is beyond the human capacity of most individuals to offer child care 24 hours a day, 7 days a week. If your policy is to offer 24-hour care, you must be certain that appropriate staff is available to support you. Generally, we accept 40 hours a week as realistic for workers in most industries. What is an appropriate work week for a child care provider?

✎ _____

## LIST RATES AND PAYMENT SCHEDULE

Clearly state the amount you will charge per hour, day, week, or month (for example, $2.50/hour, $16/day, $80/week, $300/month).

Clearly state when payment is expected (for example, on the first and fifteenth of the month, on the first and third Fridays of the month).

Require a *security deposit* or *advance payment* to protect you from parents' sudden departures without final payment. When final payment is made at the termination of the child care relationship, the advance will be refunded to parents. You can tie your advance payment policy to your notification of termination policy. For example, if you require a two-week advance notice of termination, then it makes sense to ask for an advance deposit of two weeks' payment.

Some providers choose to have *all payments made in advance.* For example, if payment is weekly, it is made at the beginning of the week. If payment is monthly, it is made at the beginning of the month. How does this policy protect a provider's income? What other businesses have similar payment policies?

✎ _____

## DESCRIBE EXPECTATIONS FOR CHILD ABSENCES

State a limited number of days per year that a child may miss, free of charge. These may be sick days, vacation days, or both. Any absence days beyond this number are paid. (We will look more closely at these policies in Chapter 4.)

State how and when you expect parents to inform you that a child will be absent (for example, a phone call by 8:30 a.m.) These are *innovator policies*. They ensure that a provider doesn't lose income when Grandma comes to town for a month or when chicken pox runs through the neighborhood. Do these policies differ from the ones you use now? How could these policies improve your profits and/or your comfort level?

✎ _____

## LIST ANY THIRD-PARTY PAYERS

*Flexible Benefits Plan:* A benefit plan offered by businesses to employees that allows employees to contribute a portion of their salary, tax-free, for the payment of dependent care expenses, out-of-pocket medical expenses, health insurance expenses, and/or retirement funds. Also known as a *cafeteria plan.*

*Cafeteria Plan:* A benefit plan offered by businesses to employees, which allows employees to contribute a portion of their salary, tax-free, for the payment of dependent care expenses, out-of-pocket medical expenses, health insurance expenses, and/or retirement funds. Also known as a *flexible benefits plan.*

Many parents receive child care payment assistance from the government or employers. Parents are often required to pay part of the child care bill. Your contract should state which portion of the child care fee will be paid by parents. Also, state whether the third party payer will pay your rate (or a predetermined hourly or daily rate) and when payment will be made. If the third party pays a rate lower than your own, you may choose to charge parents the difference.

Research the government and employer-sponsored child care payment programs in your community. Be aware of their eligibility requirements, documentation requirements, and parent co-payment requirements before you agree to participate in them. (For more information, contact your local Child Care Resource & Referral agency.)

Include in your contract a description of the parents' responsibility to complete required paperwork for third-party payment programs. Payment will be delayed if paperwork isn't turned in on time.

If customers have not fully used their employee-sponsored child care benefits by year's end in December, ask them to agree to a one-time child care fee or provider bonus. Parents may have the option to set aside child care payment from their paycheck through a **flexible benefits** (or **cafeteria) plan.** In these systems, parents must decide at the beginning of the calendar year how much they wish to set aside for child care. This amount cannot be changed during the calendar year unless very specific employment or family conditions change. If parents overestimate the amount of child care they will use, their employers get to keep any leftover money. With a year-end child care fee or bonus the provider, rather than the employer, will be the beneficiary of the parents' error. What would be a good use for a one-time year-end child care payment?

✎ _____

## LIST YOUR TERMINATION OF CONTRACT POLICY

State the necessary advance notice of termination of contract (for example, two weeks or one month). How does this policy protect provider income?

✎ _____

Some providers build a "get acquainted" period into their contracts (for example, two to six weeks). This allows both the parents and the provider time to determine whether the child care arrangement is best for the child. During this period either the parents or the provider may terminate the contract without penalty.

## LIST PENALTY FEES

State the consequences for contract violations, building compensation for inconveniences into your rates. For example, many providers charge a *late pickup fee* by the minute or quarter hour. Providers often charge an *overtime fee* at a higher rate of pay for hours worked in addition to those contracted hours. It is legitimate to charge an additional *service fee* when payment is late.

Does it bother you when a dad is chronically late to pick up his child at the end of the day or when a mom forgets to bring her checkbook on your payday? How would a written contract, signed by parents, help you enforce your policies?

✎ _____

What communication skills would help you enforce your policies?

✎ _____

## LIST SUPPLEMENTAL FEES

You may charge a *supplemental fee* for costly extra features of your service (for example, transportation, arts and crafts supplies, music lesson tutor, field trips), for an annual cost (liability insurance), or as a one-time registration fee to new families. We will talk more about supplemental fees in Chapter 4.

## SPECIFY PROVIDER LEAVE DAYS

List the holidays during which your business will not be open. These are paid holidays, calculated into your fee structure. On which holidays would you like your business to be closed?

✎ _____

✎ _____

     Your contract should list the days during which you will take your vacation leave this year. State either that you will provide a substitute or that parents are responsible for finding alternative care. If you had two weeks of paid vacation this year, when would you take them?

✎ _____

✎ _____

     State what you will do when you are sick (for example, you will call the night before so that parents can make alternative arrangements or you will hire a substitute). If you build the costs of your absence into your budget and your fee structure, you can have paid vacation and sick leave. List some reasons why child care providers should have paid leave each year.

✎ _____

✎ _____

## SPECIFY SUBSTITUTE CARE ARRANGEMENTS

State that you agree to arrange substitute care for your leave days (vacation and sick) or that parents agree to arrange their own alternative care. List possible arrangements you (or parents) could make to provide a dependable substitute for your planned and unplanned absences.

✎ _____

✎ _____

## RENEGOTIATE REGULARLY

Plan to renegotiate your contracts regularly. This creates an opportunity to reexamine your rates and fees in light of business expenses, profit margin, and market trends. Ask for parent feedback before redrafting your contract and policies, seeking parents' suggestions and concerns. Do not be afraid to raise your rates periodically, as long as your rates fall within the range of your market. Name some other businesses that renegotiate their agreements with customers or change their rates and services.

## ATTACH EMERGENCY MEDICAL INFORMATION/ RELEASE FORM

Attach to your contract a form with parents' signed permission to seek health care treatment for their child in case of a medical emergency, including the following:

- ✔ names of the child's physician and dentist
- ✔ health insurance coverage
- ✔ special disabilities, medical conditions, or dietary information necessary for management of an emergency situation (for example, allergies or medications)
- ✔ name of an alternative emergency contact whom you can call if parents can not be reached

A folder containing these forms should accompany all field trips or child transportation. Also, keep the forms ready to take to the hospital or clinic with the child if emergency medical care is needed. If you do not have a completed Emergency Medical Information/ Release Form for every child in your care, phone your Child Care Resource & Referral agency to find out how to get one.

## ATTACH A SICK CHILD EXCLUSION POLICY

Attach to your contract a *Sick Child Exclusion Policy*, a list of symptoms and conditions indicating that a child has a communicable disease. State clearly that parents are responsible for enlisting alternative care for sick children. A Sick Child Exclusion Policy should be available from your local Child Care Resource & Referral agency or Public Health Department.

Why should children with communicable diseases be excluded from well-child care settings?

✎ _____

✎ _____

✎ _____

"Your policies should fit your personality! A new provider may need to get some child care experience before he learns the optimal work conditions for his business."

# Role-Play

✔ Role-play a phone call from a provider to a parent who hurriedly dropped off a child with a fever of 101 degrees this morning.

✔ Role-play a provider telling a parent about the upcoming changes in her pricing policies and collection practices.

"It was scary the first time we renegotiated our contract. We thought we'd make our customers mad. But most of them were very understanding and saw that we were becoming more professional. That one family that left in a huff? We've never missed 'em!"

## Homework Assignment

✔ Review the model contract policy statement in Appendix A.

✔ Complete the child care contract at the end of this chapter, selecting the policies that best fit your business.

✔ Ask your local CCR&R, or public health departments, for a Sick Child Exclusion Policy you can attach to your contract.

# Notice of Contract Changes

January 2, 2XXX

Dear Parents,

Happy New Year! As owner of Play Place Family Child Care, my first priority is to provide your beautiful children with a loving, stable environment that nurtures their healthy development. And as an early childhood professional, I am committed to continuing my own education to ensure the quality of care at Play Place.

This past fall I completed a course of study in Child Care Business Skills. The course taught me how to professionalize my child care business practices, improve my record-keeping skills, and plan for the financial future of my business.

After careful consideration, I am revising some of my business policies. Changes will include monthly pre-payment, limited unscheduled child absences, a slightly increased charge for part-time care, and updated health and immunization records. I will also schedule a two-week summer vacation for myself, during which I will hire a qualified substitute.

These changes will become effective on March 1. I will soon be distributing my new contract and policy statement for your feedback. Please let me hear your feelings and opinions concerning these changes. I am committed to working with you to make the transition as stress-free as possible.

Every change I am making reflects my improved understanding of the child care industry and our local child care market. And every change will help me to guarantee consistent, high-quality care for your children. Thank you for your understanding on this matter!

Sincerely,

Xue Vang

Play Place Family Child Care

# Child Care Contract

Program Name _____

Name of Parent(s) or Guardian(s) _____

Name of Child Enrolled _____ Birth Date _____

Address _____ City _____

State _____ ZIP Code _____ Phone Number _____

Name, Address, Phone of Adults with Whom You Agree to Work

_____

_____

_____

Days and Hours of Reserved Care _____

_____

Rates and Payment Schedule _____

_____

Scheduled and Unscheduled Child Absences _____

_____

Third-Party Payers _____

_____

Termination Policy _____

_____

Penalty Fees _____

_____

Supplemental Fees _____

Provider Leave (Holiday, Vacation, Sick) _____

Substitute Care Arrangements _____

Date of Contract Renegotiation _____

*Attached:* Emergency Medical Information/Release Form

✔ name and telephone number of child's physician

✔ name and telephone number of child's dentist

✔ health insurance policy number

✔ special disabilities, medical conditions, or dietary information

✔ alternative emergency contact name and telephone number

*Attached:* Sick Child Exclusion Policy

# 3

# Eliminate Guilt!

Guilt can be a nagging menace to a nurturing person who works in a helping profession. Providers witness family struggles at close range, making it difficult not to step in as a rescuer. For example, the needs of families with young children are immense. Many parents are single, and they are often far from the support of extended family. Two paychecks may not even be enough to lift a family with young children out of poverty.

It is common for providers to feel guilty when their lives are in better circumstances than those of their customers. Providers also feel guilty when they choose not to accommodate specific needs or desires of parents.

What types of situations might inspire guilt in a child care provider?

> **Note!**
>
> Feelings of guilt have little productive value for your child care business.

✎ _____

✎ _____

✎ _____

✎ _____

✎ _____

✎ _____

✎ _____

✎ _____

# Role-Play

To gain a new perspective on situations like these, role-play the response that other professionals would give in the same circumstances.

✔ You confront your doctor, accusing her of charging you too much and telling her that you know she recently purchased a new television and VCR.

✔ You ask your grocer to open the store early for you next Saturday because you and your spouse have plans to go skiing that day.

✔ You become angry with your seven-year-old's teacher, who has gently suggested that your child be tested for dyslexia.

✔ You let your hairstylist know how unfair his recent cost increase is because your boss did not give you a raise this year.

## SET PROFESSIONAL BOUNDARIES

Providers are warm, nurturing people who love for a living. The affinities and attachments that they form with children and parents are a rewarding part of child care work. The appropriate boundaries between the professional child care provider and families can become blurred by so much day-to-day, intimate contact. Here are some points to consider:

✔ Do view yourself as a trained professional, offering a vital service to families.

✔ Do not allow your relationships with families to become cold, hardhearted, or insensitive.

✔ Do interact with parents in a respectful, professional manner.

✔ Do not try to be the child or parent's savior, family member, or close personal friend.

✔ Do set limits on the amount of services that you can provide, and be clear on the costs of those services.

✔ Do not feel guilty when your professional services cannot meet all the needs of families.

✔ Do learn to talk comfortably about the high-quality services that you provide and why they are a good value to your customers.

## HEALTHY RELATIONSHIPS ARE RESPECTFUL OF OURSELVES AND OTHERS

It is important that providers reflect occasionally on the nature of their relationship with the families and children they serve. Have you allowed some relationships with customers to become too personal, too dependent, too passive, or too irritating? If so, you may have to redefine the relationship through clear, assertive communication and behavior.

Give examples of provider comments that indicate an unhealthy professional relationship with families.

"Beware of guilt—it's a habit that is hard to break!"

✎ _____

✎ _____

✎ _____

✎ _____

✎ _____

"It's not realistic to think that you can meet all the needs of the families that you serve. Talk to another provider—she'll know how you feel."

What are some hazards of providing child care for close friends or family members?

✎ _____

✎ _____

✎ _____

✎ _____

✎ _____

# CHAPTER

# 4

## BUSINESS LESSON

# Rates, Fees, and Collection

Unlike other industries, child care profits cannot be increased through increased customer sales. In child care businesses, health and safety regulations limit the numbers of customers you can serve. With sound policies, consistent practices, and understanding of the prices the market will bear, however, many providers create a profitable small business.

## KNOW YOUR MARKET

Study your **market,** and set your rates at the middle to high end of the price range. Ask these questions:

✔ How much do other providers charge?

✔ What kinds of fee structures are now common in your community: hourly, daily, weekly, or monthly?

✔ Are certain types of child care, like infant care, weekend care, or part-time care, generally more expensive?

✔ Do prices vary between geographical areas? For example, is downtown care generally more expensive than care in outlying rural areas?

List three potential sources of market information in your community.

✎ _____

✎ _____

✎ _____

> **Note!**
>
> Pricing is a science— and an art! Research the local market, consider expenses, and set income goals before you choose your rates, fees, and collection practices.

*Market:* The individuals or businesses most likely to purchase a product or service.

Your local Child Care Resource & Referral agency can give you some perspective on your local child care market. A **market survey** may have been conducted for public information by the CCR&R, your state regulatory department, or your local child care provider association. The best way for a provider to research local prices is by calling the CCR&R or another oversight agency. If two or more providers agree on what price to charge, even through an informal discussion, they can be accused of **price fixing** in violation of the Federal Antitrust Act.

## Market Rate Survey Chart

| Number of Providers | Daily Rates | | | | | |
|---|---|---|---|---|---|---|
| | $10 | $12 | $14 | $16 | $18 | $20 |
| 20 | | | | • | | |
| 15 | | • | • | | | |
| 10 | • | | | | • | |
| 5 | | | | | | |
| 0 | | | | | | • |

"A successful small business prices its product at the middle mark or above."

To compare different prices, make a simple graph of your market that compares the numbers of providers who charge various rates. For an example, see the Market Rate Survey Chart.

## KNOW YOUR EXPENSES

Calculate your expenses before you set your rates. Just as if you were running a dry-cleaning service, a convenience food store, or a hair-styling salon, you must know how much it will cost you to do business. Then you can estimate how much you need to charge your customers.

# Brainstorming

Make a list of child care business expenses. Include categories of *fixed expenses* (or *operating expenses*) like rent, utilities, and insurance; and *variable expenses* (or *direct expenses*), which change with the number of children in your care, like food and supplies, provider wages, leave time, benefits; and business debt.

✎ _____

✎ _____

✎ _____

✎ _____

✎ _____

✎ _____

✎ _____

✎ _____

✎ _____

✎ _____

✎ _____

✎ _____

✎ _____

## INCLUDE A PROFIT GOAL

Decide your **profit goal,** the amount of money you hope to earn beyond your wages and benefits, on average, by the month and by the year. Do you need to earn enough to support your family, are you supplementing your spouse's income, or are you in business purely for fun? Although some months' expenses will be higher (and profits lower) than others, these fluctuations should be anticipated and factored into your cash flow projection.

Name your average annual and monthly profit goals.

*Profit Goal:* The amount of profit the owner expects the business to produce in a given time period.

✎ _____

## PROJECT REALISTIC NUMBERS

Build in a *vacancy estimate* of at least 10 percent in your income projections. This ensures that your budget will recognize that you cannot count on your business to have a perpetually full roster. You want to budget conservatively so that you don't find yourself over-spent during transition periods like summertime, start-up, or times of customer turnover.

Why do you think small business counselors would recommend this budget strategy to child care providers?

✎ _____

In what situations should a provider project a vacancy estimate greater than 10 percent?

✎ _____

## CONSIDER A SPECIALTY NICHE

*Niche:* A highly defined service tailored to a particular set of customers. Also known as *just what they are looking for!*

Fill a *specialty* **niche** by offering a specialized service, designed to meet a specific need of your child care market. Certain types of care may be in greater demand than others (for example, infant care, evening care, or school-age care). If you live near a large employer (the hospital, the university, the mill, or the mall) you should consider their workers' hard-to-meet child care needs (for example, shift care or part-time care).

---

### EXAMPLES

✔ Maria is an elementary school librarian who offers a before- and after-school program. Her care includes breakfast before school, walking children to and from school, assistance to children during unexpected school-day crises (like forgotten field trip money or lost mittens), and help with homework after school.

✔ Ty lives in a neighborhood near a large state university. She specializes in part-time care, and she has learned to integrate the care of children with special needs into her high-quality program. Her services are geared to customers who need only part-day child care and have high expectations of professional quality. Most of her customers are non-traditional students, university staff, and faculty.

✔ Monika offers a preschool program that includes transportation to and from weekly gymnastics classes.

✔ The international Preschool offers full-time and part-time child care that includes daily age-appropriate language activities in French, German, and Spanish.

---

In your community, which types of care are in greater demand than others?

✎ _____

## FULL-TIME VERSUS PART-TIME

Choose a payment rate that adequately compensates you for part-time care. In most markets, part-time care costs more than full-time care. It is often a provider's preference to work with only full-time customers because the work involves fewer schedule changes, less billing, less record keeping, and fewer children. Part-time care, though, is often in great demand, and it may not be profitable for a provider to rule it out of her business.

What are the advantages and disadvantages of offering only full-time care?

✎ _____

✎ _____

What are the advantages of offering part-time care?

✎ _____

Why would a provider charge a higher fee for part-time rather than full-time care?

✎ _____

Charge a *minimum rate* for part-time care. For example, a daily minimum might be four hours. If a family uses only three hours/day, they pay the minimum rate for four hours/day. The minimum rate may be defined in hours/day, hours/week, days/week, or days or hours/month.

Set a *maximum number of hours* for full-time care. For example, if the maximum is eight hours, a family would pay a supplemental hourly fee when they used nine or more hours/day.

## PAID CHILD ABSENCES

Charge for reserved care whether it is used or not. When a provider sets aside a slot for a child in her care, she is making a commitment not to market that slot to any other customer. The parent has paid to have that slot reserved, whether or not the child uses it.

How does this policy protect the provider from unplanned loss of income?

✎ _____

> "Specialty niches generally command a higher-than-average price."

Limit the number of absences for which parents will not be charged (for example, to 10 days/year). After these are used, for any reason (vacation, illness, family visitors) charge for the reserved time.

## BEWARE OF FAMILY RATES

Do not lose your profit margin when offering a *family rate*. Sit down with pencil and paper and compute the difference in income your discount rates will create. Consider your market goals and market conditions before implementing discount rates.

---

### EXAMPLES
Here are four different family rates, calculated for a daily rate of $15:

✔ Provider 1 offers a 33 percent discount for the second child and a 66 percent discount for the third child. Her total annual income for the care of three children is $7,560.

✔ Provider 2 offers a 20 percent discount for the second child and a 30 percent discount for the third child. Her total annual income for the care of three children is $9,456.

✔ Provider 3 offers a 10 percent discount for the second and third child. Her total annual income for the care of three children is $10,584.

✔ Provider 4 offers no family discounts and earns $11,700/year.

---

Why might a provider choose not to offer any family rates?

✎ _____

"Never institute a new policy until you have run the numbers!"

## SUPPLEMENTAL FEES

Charge supplemental fees as necessary to meet the expenses of program operation. Review your services to make sure you are covering all of the costs you incur for example, if you offer transportation, do your fees cover the costs of vehicle maintenance, insurance, and fuel?

List some of the costly extra features for which a child care service might charge a supplemental fees.

✎ _____

Providers may pass along large annual or one-time expenses to parents (for example, an annual insurance premium or facility improvement). Recurring or ongoing expenses, however, should be built into new rates. List some one-time expenses that a provider might pass along to parents.

✎ _____

## PAYMENT SCHEDULES

Time your payment schedule to work for your business. For example, payment might be weekly, biweekly, or monthly. If end-of-month payment makes it difficult for you to pay your bills on time, consider asking for payment in advance. When changing payment schedules, give parents advance warning in writing.

What are the advantages of a monthly payment schedule? Of an advance payment schedule?

✎ _____

Consider a flat monthly rate.

---

### EXAMPLE

Blossom's Child Care customers are either part time (minimum of 4 hours/day) or full time (more than 4 hours/day). All customers pay a flat rate based on 21 days/month, every month. It is true that some months are 1 or 2 working days longer, but Blossom feels that her fees are fair and easy to calculate. Further, Blossom does not give parents a discount when their children are absent. Parents accept this policy when they understand that she provides several days of "free" care during the longer months.

---

## BUILD IN A RAISE

Review and revise rates regularly. You are like many other workers if you expect an increase in pay on an annual schedule, but this understanding must be reflected in your contract language. Raises may be tied to expanded services or increased levels of training.

Many workers receive a **cost-of-living adjustment (COLA)** based on this year's economic trends as measured by the federal government. This, too, must be reflected in your contract language. You can call your local office of the Social Security Administration to learn this year's COLA.

If you are changing your policies for the first time, you must send a letter to your customers explaining your business decision and describing why the change is necessary to ensure high-quality, stable care for children. Then make yourself available to talk about your policy changes.

How would you explain to parents your decision to implement an annual raise?

✎ _____

*Cost-of-Living Adjustment (COLA):* A change in salary or wage, based on the annual federal government's cost-of-living index. Many employers review the cost of living on an annual basis and adjust employee wages accordingly.

---

"As I said, most parents were completely supportive when we changed our policies. They liked the improved professionalism and stability of our child care. The few that left were not parents whom we wished to keep!"

## Brainstorming

Comment on this statement: "Some observers of the child care industry have remarked that it is the only business they know where veteran workers make less than newcomers to the profession." True or false?

✐ _____

✐ _____

✐ _____

✐ _____

✐ _____

✐ _____

✐ _____

List some ideas to help parents transition smoothly into new policies.

✐ _____

✐ _____

✐ _____

## BE SURE TO BREAK EVEN

*Break-Even Analysis:* A calculation of the level of sales necessary to pay all costs.

A provider's income should cover her costs! Before you make a final decision regarding your contract obligations, rates, and fees, ask yourself, "How much will I have to earn per child to offset my expenses?" A **break-even analysis** evaluates your potential to cover costs and reach profit goals. Complete this simple break even analysis. In order to break even at an average enrollment rate of 90 percent, you may need to adjust your fees.

# Break-Even Analysis

**Monthly Direct Costs** (Expenses that depend on the number of children you serve)

Food . . . . . . . . . . . . . . . . . . . . . . . . . . . . . . . . . . . . . . . . . . . . . . . . . . . . . $ _____

Materials . . . . . . . . . . . . . . . . . . . . . . . . . . . . . . . . . . . . . . . . . . . . . . . . . $ _____

Labor . . . . . . . . . . . . . . . . . . . . . . . . . . . . . . . . . . . . . . . . . . . . . . . . . . . . $ _____

Plus

**Monthly Operating Costs** (These expenses don't vary month to month)

Advertising . . . . . . . . . . . . . . . . . . . . . . . . . . . . . . . . . . . . . . . . . . . . . . . $ _____

Arts and Crafts Supplies . . . . . . . . . . . . . . . . . . . . . . . . . . . . . . . . . . . . . $ _____

Dues/Subscriptions . . . . . . . . . . . . . . . . . . . . . . . . . . . . . . . . . . . . . . . . . $ _____

Insurance . . . . . . . . . . . . . . . . . . . . . . . . . . . . . . . . . . . . . . . . . . . . . . . . . $ _____

Maintenance/Repairs . . . . . . . . . . . . . . . . . . . . . . . . . . . . . . . . . . . . . . . . $ _____

Office Supplies . . . . . . . . . . . . . . . . . . . . . . . . . . . . . . . . . . . . . . . . . . . . . $ _____

Rent . . . . . . . . . . . . . . . . . . . . . . . . . . . . . . . . . . . . . . . . . . . . . . . . . . . . . $ _____

Telephone . . . . . . . . . . . . . . . . . . . . . . . . . . . . . . . . . . . . . . . . . . . . . . . . $ _____

Wages (For staff who don't work directly with children) . . . . . . . . . $ _____

Training . . . . . . . . . . . . . . . . . . . . . . . . . . . . . . . . . . . . . . . . . . . . . . . . . . $ _____

Other . . . . . . . . . . . . . . . . . . . . . . . . . . . . . . . . . . . . . . . . . . . . . . . . . . . . $ _____

Plus

**Other Cash Needs** (Debt payment, taxes) . . . . . . . . . . . . . . . . . . . . . . $ _____

Plus

**Profit Goal** (Your decision) . . . . . . . . . . . . . . . . . . . . . . . . . . . . . . . . . . $ _____

Equals

**Break-Even Point** . . . . . . . . . . . . . . . . . . . . . . . . . . . . . . . . . . . . . . . . . $ _____

Now calculate:

**Break-Even Point** . . . . . . . . . . . . . . . . . . . . . . . . . . . . . . . . . . . . . . . . . $ _____

**Divided by Number of Children Served Per Month**
(Limited by state regulations) . . . . . . . . . . . . . . . . . . . . . . . . . . . . . . . . . $ _____

Equals

**Average Monthly Income Needed Per Child** . . . . . . . . . . . . . . . . . . $ _____

# LEARN TO HANDLE PRICING OBJECTIONS

Understand parents' concerns when they ask about prices. Child care is the average American family's fourth largest expense—after housing, food, and taxes! Child care for one child can easily cost 33 percent of a working parent's income. Multiplying a provider's rate by the number of children in her care can give a false impression of a high provider income. What parents don't usually understand is how much it costs to offer quality care.

Providers must be comfortable talking about their business expenses and about why their service is valuable. Talk value! Many parents do not know how to recognize value in a child care setting. You must educate your customers. Features such as availability of care, a healthy and safe environment, individual attention, low adult-to-child ratio, nutritious meals and snacks, age-appropriate materials and equipment, developmentally appropriate daily curriculum, a well-trained provider, and a highly communicative provider all indicate high-quality care and are valuable to parents.

What kinds of concerns do parents have when they object to child care prices?

✎ _____

✎ _____

✎ _____

✎ _____

✎ _____

Plan and rehearse the response you will give when parents bring up their pricing concerns. Describe the traits of quality child care; list the benefits that your child care service offers a child; and illustrate examples of the unique qualities of your business. And don't leave the topic of pricing until the parent is comfortable. Close the deal— get a commitment that they understand your pricing policies.

✔ "I know child care is a big expense for families today, and it's not easy for you to absorb a rate increase. When I researched our local child care market, I found that my new rates are well within the range for infant care in our town. Infant care is very hard to find. Infants need more individualized attention than older children, and I guarantee a low ratio of children to adults in my child care. I also provide nourishing meals and disposable diapers at no extra charge."

✔ "What you are paying for is the guarantee that your baby will get individualized attention all day long, that my facility is safe and pleasant for her, and that the activities we do each day will support her mental, physical, and emotional development."

✔ "My rates are higher than those of some of the other child care providers in the neighborhood, but that is because I have an Associate's degree in child development, and my facility is accredited by the National Association of Home Child Care."

✔ "Now you understand that a rate increase is necessary to cover my monthly business expenses. Are you comfortable with my new contract now?"

## Role-Play

Modeling your response on the examples given previously, role-play a provider discussing her rates with a prospective parent customer.

"Believe you're worth it, and back it up!"

"Need to learn to talk value? Practice with a friend."

✔ Using the "Child Care Business Expenses" worksheet at the end of this chapter, list your child care business expenses. Refer to recent bills and receipts, and if necessary estimate your costs.

✔ Complete the "Break-Even Analysis" worksheet at the end of this chapter, estimating the number of children you must serve each month to cover expenses and make a profit. Can you break even when you project a 90 percent enrollment rate, or do you need to adjust your fees?

✔ Write one brief paragraph describing your business. Include services offered, years in business, your training, and anything that describes the high-quality value of your business compared to other child care businesses.

✔ Write one brief paragraph describing how your contract and policies support the profitability of your business.

## Market Rate Survey Worksheet

Completed on _____, 20__

| Number of Providers | Daily Rates | | | | | |
|---|---|---|---|---|---|---|
| | $10 | $12 | $14 | $16 | $18 | $20 |
| 20 | | | | | | |
| 15 | | | | | | |
| 10 | | | | | | |
| 5 | | | | | | |
| 0 | | | | | | |
| | | | | | | |

# Child Care Business Expense Worksheet

## (Annual or Monthly)

| Expense Category | Expense |
|---|---|
| Personnel | |
| ✔ Provider Wages | _____ |
| ✔ Provider Taxes | _____ |
| ✔ Provider Benefits | _____ |
| Food | _____ |
| Supplies | _____ |
| Child Activity Materials | _____ |
| Child Care Equipment | _____ |
| Child Care Furniture | _____ |
| Facility Occupancy | _____ |
| Facility Utilities | _____ |
| Facility Maintenance/Repair | _____ |
| Telephone | _____ |
| Training Fees | _____ |
| Subscriptions/Memberships | _____ |
| Loan Payment | _____ |
| Substitute Care | _____ |
| Accountant Services | _____ |
| Bank Fees | _____ |
| Other: | _____ |
| Other: | _____ |
| Other: | _____ |
| Other: | _____ |

# Break-Even Analysis

**Monthly Direct Costs** (Expenses that depend on the number of children you serve)

Food . . . . . . . . . . . . . . . . . . . . . . . . . . . . . . . . . . . . . . . . . . . . . $ _____

Materials . . . . . . . . . . . . . . . . . . . . . . . . . . . . . . . . . . . . . . . . . . $ _____

Labor . . . . . . . . . . . . . . . . . . . . . . . . . . . . . . . . . . . . . . . . . . . . . $ _____

Plus

**Monthly Operating Costs** (These expenses don't vary month to month)

Advertising . . . . . . . . . . . . . . . . . . . . . . . . . . . . . . . . . . . . . . . . $ _____

Arts and Crafts Supplies . . . . . . . . . . . . . . . . . . . . . . . . . . . . . . . $ _____

Dues/Subscriptions . . . . . . . . . . . . . . . . . . . . . . . . . . . . . . . . . . $ _____

Insurance . . . . . . . . . . . . . . . . . . . . . . . . . . . . . . . . . . . . . . . . . . $ _____

Maintenance/Repairs . . . . . . . . . . . . . . . . . . . . . . . . . . . . . . . . . $ _____

Office Supplies . . . . . . . . . . . . . . . . . . . . . . . . . . . . . . . . . . . . . . $ _____

Rent . . . . . . . . . . . . . . . . . . . . . . . . . . . . . . . . . . . . . . . . . . . . . . $ _____

Telephone . . . . . . . . . . . . . . . . . . . . . . . . . . . . . . . . . . . . . . . . . $ _____

Wages (For staff who don't work directly with children) . . . . . . . . . $ _____

Training . . . . . . . . . . . . . . . . . . . . . . . . . . . . . . . . . . . . . . . . . . . $ _____

Other . . . . . . . . . . . . . . . . . . . . . . . . . . . . . . . . . . . . . . . . . . . . . $ _____

Plus

**Other Cash Needs** (Debt payment, taxes) . . . . . . . . . . . . . . . . . . . . . $ _____

Plus

**Profit Goal** (Your decision) . . . . . . . . . . . . . . . . . . . . . . . . . . . . . . . $ _____

Equals

**Break-Even Point** . . . . . . . . . . . . . . . . . . . . . . . . . . . . . . . . . . . . . . $ _____

Now calculate:

**Break-Even Point** . . . . . . . . . . . . . . . . . . . . . . . . . . . . . . . . . . . . . . $ _____
**Divided by Number of Children Served Per Month**
(Limited by state regulations) . . . . . . . . . . . . . . . . . . . . . . . . . . . . . $ _____

Equals

**Average Monthly Income Needed Per Child** . . . . . . . . . . . . . . . . . . $ _____

# 5

## COMMUNICATION LESSON

# Communication Styles: Passive, Aggressive, and Assertive

Every time we communicate with other people, we choose from a range of behavior styles. This choice reflects our attitudes about other people's actions, thoughts, feelings, and human rights. This choice might reflect the situation in which you find yourself at a specific moment, the person with whom you are talking, the topic of your discussion, or the environment of your setting. Sometimes the choice is conscious; sometimes it is automatic.

Nobody exhibits passive or aggressive behaviors exclusively. The most aggressive boss may be a fearful pussycat underneath. Or the mildest-mannered convenience store cashier may actually be seething with anger and manipulation inside. Our cultural literature is full of characters who epitomize the extremes of communication styles. You will notice that they usually work in pairs—passive and aggressive: They need each other's complementary behavior for their strategies to work. If you are engaged in a struggle with a passive or aggressive communicator, check to make sure you are not playing the opposite role. If you are, one way to create change is to *change your own behavior first!*

> **Note!**
>
> An assertive communication style is most likely to lead to productive outcomes for your business.

## PASSIVE COMMUNICATION STYLE

Here are some attitudes and behaviors that are characteristic of passiveness.

- ✔ You are OK, but I am not. I am not confident in myself.
- ✔ I let other people make decisions for me . . . I don't want to take risks.

"When I was just starting my child care, I was not comfortable with my role as a business owner. My nature is easy-going, flexible, and generous. But I have learned to use a more direct approach when I am talking with parents. It helps me to communicate more effectively and to enforce my policies."

✔ I ignore my own needs and desires, but I satisfy the needs and desires of others.

✔ I am uncomfortable sharing my feelings and opinions. What do I know, anyway?

✔ I am comfortable in the roles of Victim and Martyr, and I feel better when others pity me.

✔ If I suffer enough, people will admire me.

Can you add to this list? Can you think of times when you may choose to behave in an outwardly passive manner, but you do not conform to the attitudes listed here?

Name some characters from popular television shows, books, or movies who demonstrate the traits of passive behavior.

✎ _____

## Role-Play

Role-play this child care scenario. A parent has not paid her child care bill on time in two months. Behaving very passively, the provider tries to discuss this unacceptable situation with the mom at pick-up time on Friday night.

## AGGRESSIVE COMMUNICATION STYLE

Some people think they are behaving aggressively, when in fact they are behaving assertively. It is helpful to remember that aggression is disrespectful and manipulative. Aggression is mean-spirited! Here are some attitudes and behaviors that are characteristic of aggressiveness.

✔ I am OK, but you are not.

✔ I act very confident in myself . . . but deep inside I do not feel confident.

✔ I control and dominate other people so that I can have things my way.

✔ I need to feel superior to other people so, compared to me, you are stupid, lazy, or worthless.

✔ I believe I know what is best and right for other people so I will gladly make your decisions for you.

✔ I get what I want, through intimidation, charisma, force, or coercion—whether you want it or not!

Can you add to this list? How do these traits compare to those of the passive communicator? Are they based on different principles or similar ones? How does a person who is behaving aggressively deal with making a mistake, being criticized, or changing his or her mind?

Name some characters from popular television shows, books, or movies who demonstrate the traits of aggressive behavior.

✎ _____

## Role-Play

A parent has arranged in advance to be late picking up his child tonight because it is the night of his company's annual holiday party. When he shows up, the provider suspects that he is too intoxicated to drive. Role-play the provider's aggressive response.

## PASSIVE-AGGRESSIVE COMMUNICATION STYLE

This approach is always used secretly. Sometimes the secrecy is based in mean-spirited dishonesty. Sometimes it is caused by societal limitations that won't allow the person to openly exert authority or control in the situation. It is often the course of action chosen by a determined underdog (for example, an ambitious woman in a very traditional, male-dominated environment). Can you think of other examples? If someone is giving you the passive-aggressive treatment, you have to bring the situation out of the shadows and eliminate all secrecy. Here are some attitudes and behaviors that are characteristic of passive-aggressiveness.

- ✔ I am OK and you are not, but I won't let you know I think this about you.
- ✔ I control and dominate other people, but I do it secretly.
- ✔ I need to feel superior to others, but I do not want them to know that I think they aren't as virtuous, intelligent, or valuable as I am.
- ✔ I believe I know what is best for other people, so I like to make their decisions for them, secretly.
- ✔ I manipulate situations from behind the scenes, through deception and secrecy.

Is this behavior pattern similar to passiveness, aggressiveness, or both? How does a person who is behaving passive-aggressively deal with making a mistake, being criticized, or changing his mind? Name some characters from popular television shows, books, or movies who demonstrate the traits of passive-aggressive behavior.

✎ _____

# Role-Play

A provider is unhappy with a new child care customer, a four-year-old who has been in the child care setting for three long, unpleasant weeks. The child has bitten other children, thrown tantrums at every lunchtime, and been generally disruptive to the daily routine. The provider doesn't really like this child's parents, either. But they are her husband's boss's in-laws, and she doesn't want to be the one to terminate the relationship. Role-play the provider's passive-aggressive behavior.

## ASSERTIVE COMMUNICATION STYLE

You can see how the previous three communication styles are all based on a similar set of principles that assumes people are not equal or entitled to equal treatment; that some people's opinions don't matter as much as others; and if you aren't a winner you will be a loser. What a different value system underlies assertive behavior! Here are some attitudes and behaviors that are characteristic of assertiveness.

✔ I am OK, you are OK.
✔ I do not believe there must be a hierarchy of winners and losers.
✔ I believe that power can be shared.
✔ I respect my own rights and the rights of others.
✔ I voice my opinions and feelings.
✔ I listen respectfully to the opinions and feelings of others.
✔ I make my own decisions, and I am willing to experience the consequences.
✔ I do make mistakes sometimes.
✔ I also change my mind now and then.
✔ I give criticism constructively.

✔ I listen to destructive criticism and try to learn from it, but I do not necessarily agree.

✔ I know I am not perfect, but I still I have confidence in myself.

✔ I value negotiation and compromise.

✔ I try to let go of issues beyond my control.

✔ I take care of myself physically, emotionally, and professionally.

When you are behaving assertively, you are not on auto-pilot. In other words, you are not reacting with a certain behavior because it is comfortable or because it is what other people expect of you. Sometimes the best way to determine whether a behavior is assertive is to look at the underlying assumptions and motivations.

Name some characters from popular television shows, books, or movies who demonstrate the traits of assertive behavior.

✎ _____

## Role-Play

A provider has been in business for five years. He enjoys an excellent reputation for offering quality care, and he rarely has vacancies. His families have been with him for a long time, and he knows them well. For the first time ever, he wants to raise his rates. Some of the parents live on a very tight budget, and they will be unhappy when they hear this news. Role-play the provider as he assertively informs the parents of the rate change.

## STEREOTYPES

Sometimes these communication or behavior styles become culturally associated with different groups of people. For example, female servants in households of the Victorian era were expected to behave passively, while Hell's Angels motorcycle club members of the 1960s were supposed to behave aggressively.

How would you describe the culturally stereotyped behaviors expected of people who provide care for children? How does this stereotype conflict with your role as a business manager?

✎ _____

✎ _____

✎ _____

**"Smart cookie!"**

## ADVANTAGES OF ASSERTIVENESS

None of these communication styles is always "right" or "wrong." We try to choose the behavior that communicates our feelings most effectively or brings us a desired and predictable response. For example, if a neighborhood bully steals a child's bicycle, the child's parents might choose to respond aggressively. If a well-meaning husband horribly burns the dinner he has lovingly prepared for his wife's birthday, she may very well choose to respond passively.

An assertive style is recommended for communication between provider and parents because it conveys an attitude of respectfulness. An assertive communication style also helps a child care provider communicate and enforce business policies more effectively. Assertive listening helps a provider to learn more about the parents and children with whom he works. And an assertive child care provider has fewer problems asking for feedback, admitting a mistake, or changing his mind.

## ASSERTIVENESS IS A SKILL

Babies are the most assertive people you will ever meet. They ask for what they want and need. They express their feelings openly. They are never trying to be mean to you. You were born assertive! If you aren't behaving assertively now, it is probably because you learned other communication strategies. You can relearn assertiveness.

Practice makes perfect. Practice every day—in small interactions with parents, in role-play with a trusted friend, or in rehearsal with the rear-view mirror while you wait at a traffic light. It will become easier the more often you do it. Not only will you become more comfortable with new patterns of self-expression, but you will experience small successes that reinforce your new behaviors.

It is a good idea, however, to make change in small increments. If you decide you have been too passive in your personal life, don't do a personality make-over this weekend. Instead, make small, manageable changes, one day at a time. Give friends and family a chance to get used to your new responses.

Listen to your feelings. If your stomach is tightening, your temples are pounding, and your blood pressure is rising, your body may be reminding you to take better care of yourself or your business.

# 6

## BUSINESS LESSON

# An Effective Record-Keeping System

A child care provider's business records are the backbone of profitability. Business records track real income and expenses. They project cash flow, and they are vital to creating a workable budget. Records document tax **deductions**. They help a business owner make effective decisions about new marketing activities, staffing patterns, and policies.

> **Note!**
>
> Your record-keeping system needs a separate checking account for your business, a monthly income and expense ledger, and a filing system.

## SEPARATE CHECKING ACCOUNT

Establish a **checking account** separate from personal checking, into which all child care income is deposited and out of which all child care business expenses are paid. Shop around among banks to get the best services and most reasonable terms available. Is there a minimum deposit? Will you be limited in the number of checks you can write each month without paying extra? Are checks free?

*Deductions:* Business operation expenses that may be used to reduce business gross profit for tax purposes.

*Checking Account:* A bank deposit against which checks can be drawn. Used to separate business income and expenses from personal income and expenses.

> **EXAMPLE**
> Rudy, a home child care provider, is at the grocery store picking up some dinner items for her family, and she remembers that she will need two cartons of milk tomorrow for the child care program. Ordinarily, she pays for weekly child care groceries with a separate check from her business account, but tonight she does not have the business checkbook with her. What should she do?

Deposit every dollar received, whether from payments or loans, into your child care checking account. Every expense incurred, including provider wages and monthly profit, should be paid by check.

## BUSINESS INCOME AND EXPENSE LEDGER

*Ledger:* A record-keeping format that records business income and expenses by category.

Track income and expenses on a monthly basis through a **business ledger**. A ledger is like an expanded check register, and it provides important information for many business decisions. The business ledger system should have three sections.

### Business Income

The first section is a record of *business income* broken down into specific categories (for example, tuition, special fees, and CACFP reimbursement).

### Deposits Made and Checks Written

The second section is similar to a checkbook register. It is a record of the date and amount of *all deposits made and checks written*.

### Business Expenses

The third section is a record of *business expenses* broken down into specific categories (for example, food, art supplies, utilities). Use the "other" column for expense categories that occur infrequently, such as professional services (attorney, CPA, consultants), professional training, bank fees, equipment.

Once the income and expense ledger for the month is completed, a provider can determine the total business income for the month, the largest source of income, total expenses for the month, and the amount spent in each expense category. What other information would the ledger reveal?

✎ _____

Balance the ledger monthly. Reconcile the business checking account with the bank statement at each month's end. The ledger and bank statement should agree. A child care business ledger tracks where money is coming from and where it is going.

## CHILD CARE LEDGER SYSTEMS

You can purchase a generic ledger book for tracking monthly income and expenses at your local office supply store. But it is helpful to use a ledger system designed specifically for child care businesses. Ask the staff at your local Child Care Resource & Referral agency for a suggestion on popular child care ledgers and where to buy them. Or check the advertisements in an early childhood magazine or journal.

## FILING SYSTEM

Keep records in a simple filing system, to provide the paper documentation that backs up the ledger. Every business requires a different type of paperwork. Here is a list of the files that a child care business should keep:

*Assets:* Value of everything owned by the business, including inventory, furniture, equipment, accounts receivable, cash, land, or property.

- ✔ alphabetical, monthly, or by category—All receipts and paid bills
- ✔ **assets**—List all furniture and equipment valued at more than $100, with purchase date and value
- ✔ bank statements—Reconciled
- ✔ child care information—Child and Adult Care Food Program records, provider training records, daily attendance records
- ✔ contracts—Child care business registration papers, liability and automobile insurance policies, lease, professional service agreements (for example, substitute care providers, snowplow, lawn care)
- ✔ customers—Filed alphabetically by children's names, to include addresses and telephone numbers, signed customer contracts, medical release forms, child immunization records
- ✔ inquiries—Waiting list of potential customers
- ✔ payables—Bills to be paid
- ✔ payroll—Documentation of employee citizenship status, tax forms, copy of hire letter stating wage and hours, records of quarterly payroll, tax payments, payroll adjustments, payroll forms
- ✔ receivables—Money owed to business
- ✔ staff—Filed alphabetically by staff names, include telephone numbers, training records, immunization records, and other regulation records
- ✔ suppliers—Catalogs and notes kept by provider about specific suppliers, services, problems encountered with certain products

# Child Care Income and Expense Ledger Exercise

Look at February's business ledger for Rainbow Home Child Care on the next page, partially completed by owner Samaya Yafai. The already completed section is a duplication of the entries from Samaya's checkbook. Complete the ledger page by following the steps below. When you are done you can check your entries against those in the Rainbow Home Child Care Ledger Key on page 46.

1. Record the amount of each deposit in the appropriate income category.
2. Record the amount of each check written in the appropriate expense category.
3. Total each income column. Add the totals of all income columns. This total should equal the total of the "Amounts of Deposits" column. Does it?
4. Total each expense column. Add the totals of all expense columns. This total should equal the total of the "Amount of Checks" column. Does it?
5. Add the Beginning Balance plus the Total Amount of Deposits. From this sum, subtract the Total Amount of Checks. Does this agree with the ledger's Ending Balance, and with Samaya's check register at the end of the month? It should!

Beginning Balance

+ Total Amount of Deposits

= 

– Total Amount of Checks

_____

= Ending Balance

When you have completed the Rainbow Home Child Care Income and Expense Ledger, give Samaya this information:

❱ the total business income for the month of February
❱ the largest source of income
❱ total expenses for the month and the amount spent in each expense category

Are her records in balance?

# ✎ Rainbow Home Child Care—Month of February, 2XXX

## Ledger Spreadsheet

| Income — Miscellaneous Descr. | Income — Miscellaneous Amt. | Child Care Tuition | USDA Food Program | Amount of Deposit | Balance | DATE | Checks Issued To & Deposit Descriptions | In Payment Of | Check # | Amount of Check | Food | Supplies—Mat'ls | Maint Repair |
|---|---|---|---|---|---|---|---|---|---|---|---|---|---|
| | | | | | 155 | | ←BROUGHT FORWARD→ | | | | | | |
| | | | | | 155 | 2-1 | Safeway | Groceries | 501 | 164 | | | |
| | | | | 600 | 566 | | Swanson, Brown | | 502 | 25 | | | |
| | | | | | | | Bill Watson | Snow Removal | | | | | |
| | | | | 800 | | 2-5 | Martin, White, Saito | | 503 | 60 | | | |
| | | | | | | | Harrington | Taxes | 504 | 15 | | | |
| | | | | | | | US WEST | Phone Bill | 505 | 30 | | | |
| | | | | | 1261 | | MT. Power | Electric Bill | 506 | 136 | | | |
| | | | | | 1100 | 2-6 | Bi-Lo Foods | Groceries | 507 | 25 | | | |
| | | | | 600 | 1700 | 2-9 | For Teachers & Kids, Etc. | Clay, markers | | | | | |
| | | | | | | | Cates, Harvey, George | | 508 | 10 | | | |
| | | | | | 1650 | | CCR&R | Workshop Fee | 509 | 40 | | | |
| | | | | | 1625 | 2-11 | Susan Harris (Sub) | Wages-4 hours | 510 | 25 | | | |
| | | | | | | 2/15 | K-Mart | Toys | — | 10 | | | |
| | | | | 320 | 1735 | | U-Bank | Service Charge | | | | | |
| | | | | | 1635 | 2-20 | USDA Food Program | | 511 | 300 | | | |
| | | | | | 435 | 2-28 | Montana Comm. Devl | Loan | 512 | 1200 | | | |
| | | | | | | | Samaya Yafai | Salary | | | | | |
| | | | | 2320 | 435 | | | | | 2040 | | | |

# Rainbow Home Child Care—Month of February, 2XXX

## Ledger Spreadsheet

| Miscellaneous Descr. | Amt. | Child Care Tuition | USDA Food Program | Amount of Deposit | Balance | DATE | Checks Issued To & Deposit Descriptions | In Payment Of | Check # | Amount of Check | Food | Supplies—Mat'ls | Maint Repair |
|---|---|---|---|---|---|---|---|---|---|---|---|---|---|
|  |  |  |  |  | 155 |  | ←BROUGHT FORWARD→ |  |  |  |  |  |  |
|  |  |  |  |  |  | 2-1 | Safeway | Groceries | 501 | 164 | 164 |  |  |
|  |  | 600 |  | 600 | 566 |  | Swanson, Brown |  |  |  |  |  |  |
|  |  |  |  |  |  |  | Bill Watson | Snow Removal | 502 | 25 |  |  | 25 |
|  |  | 800 |  | 800 |  | 2-5 | Martin, White, Saito |  |  |  |  |  |  |
|  |  |  |  |  |  |  | Harrington | Taxes | 503 | 60 |  |  |  |
|  |  |  |  |  |  |  | US WEST | Phone Bill | 504 | 15 |  |  |  |
|  |  |  |  |  | 1261 |  | MT. Power | Electric Bill | 505 | 30 |  |  |  |
|  |  |  |  |  |  | 2-6 | Bi-Lo Foods | Groceries | 506 | 136 | 136 |  |  |
|  |  |  |  |  | 1100 |  | For Teachers & Kids, Etc. | Clay, markers | 507 | 25 |  | 25 |  |
|  |  | 600 |  | 600 | 1700 | 2-9 | Cates, Harvey, George |  |  |  |  |  |  |
|  |  |  |  |  |  | 2-10 | CCR&R | Workshop Fee | 508 | 10 |  |  |  |
|  |  |  |  |  | 1650 |  | Susan Harris (Sub) | Wages-4 hours | 509 | 40 |  |  |  |
|  |  |  |  |  | 1625 | 2-11 | K-Mart | Toys | 510 | 25 |  | 25 |  |
|  |  |  |  |  |  | 2/15 | U-Bank | Service Charge | — | 10 |  |  |  |
|  |  |  | 320 | 320 | 1935 |  | USDA Food Program |  |  |  |  |  |  |
|  |  |  |  |  | 1635 | 2-20 | Montana Comm. Devl | Loan | 511 | 300 |  |  |  |
|  |  |  |  |  | 435 | 2-28 | Samaya Yafai | Salary | 512 | 1200 |  |  |  |
|  |  | 2000 | 320 | 2320 | 435 |  |  |  |  | 2040 | 300 | 50 | 25 |

✔ tickler file—Reminder list or calendar with *to-do* tasks (for example, monthly billing, quarterly insurance premium payment, annual business card printing, annual review of contract/policies)

A provider may need additional files such as inventory, curricula, project ideas, and others.

## RETAIN THESE RECORDS *PERMANENTLY:*

- ✔ municipal business license
- ✔ insurance policies
- ✔ financial statements
- ✔ accounting records
- ✔ audit reports, copies of income tax returns
- ✔ depreciation schedules
- ✔ if incorporated, corporate bylaws, minutes of stockholders meetings, and annual reports

## RETAIN THESE RECORDS FOR *SEVEN YEARS:*

- ✔ canceled checks
- ✔ payroll records
- ✔ sales vouchers and invoice details
- ✔ contracts and leases
- ✔ accounts receivable and payable

"My life is so much easier since I started using this record-keeping system. Now I know that I am on top of things. I don't worry about unexpected bills turning up, and I don't wonder if I made any money last month. I _know_ my earnings, my expenses, and my profits."
"Right on, ladies and gentlemen. Let the revolution begin!"

"If you have already done these things, congratulations! You should be a child care provider mentor."

The following activities are the backbone of any small business. If you have not already completed them, begin working on them today.

✔ Set up a checking account for your child care business.

✔ Keep a business ledger. Purchase it at the local office supply store, or order one from a child care supplier.

✔ Purchase an accordion folder and set up your filing system using the categories listed earlier.

✔ Collect the documents you need to complete your records, and store them together in a fireproof box or filing cabinet.

✔ Write one brief paragraph describing your business record-keeping system.

# 7

## COMMUNICATION LESSON

# Listening Skills

When someone criticizes you, it is hard to listen well. This is especially true when the criticism is offered in an aggressive manner. Good listening skills increase the amount of information shared and improve your understanding of the problem. They follow the same principles that guide assertive behavior. Here are some tips that will help you be a better listener.

> **Note!**
>
> Active listening leads to problem solving!

## LET YOUR ACTIONS SHOW THAT YOU CARE

Your behavior should show that you are listening. For example, an attentive listener sits up straight rather than slouches. He avoids distractions by turning off the television or closing the door. He might even lean forward toward the speaker and nod his head as he listens. List some of the other actions and *body language* that are typical of a good listener.

## GIVE SHORT, ENCOURAGING RESPONSES

Without interrupting, a good listener gives reassurance and support to the speaker. This sounds like this: "Uh-huh. Right. OK. OK. Yeah? Uh-huh. Yikes." How do you feel when you are talking to someone and getting none of this response from your listener?

## PARAPHRASE THE SPEAKER'S MESSAGE BACK TO HIM

Using your own words, describe what you heard the speaker say. This is how you verify that you heard the message correctly. It is possible you have misunderstood the issue. This strategy gives the speaker an opportunity to correct your misunderstanding before the dialogue goes any further.

---

### EXAMPLES

A father startles home provider Linda Hernandez with his demands for copies of her meal and snack menus to review at home, and he states that his daughter seems to be starving every evening when he picks her up. Linda responds, "It sounds like you've been wondering if Samantha is getting enough nutritious food at child care."

Provider Dan Harper has asked a mother repeatedly for her one-year-old's updated immunization records, but today Mom surprises Dan by stating angrily, "If other parents want to put their baby's health at risk, that's their business. I'm not going to do it!" Dan responds, "Let me see if I understand you—you would prefer not to get Joey's immunizations at this time?"

An angry neighbor has come over to the Children's Center for the third time this month to tell Director Mary Charlo that child care customers own the cars that have been blocking her driveway in the alley. Mary responds, "You are trapped by the cars blocking the alley."

---

## REFLECT THE SPEAKER'S FEELINGS BACK TO HIM

Use *feeling words* to describe the emotion that the speaker is trying to communicate. This requires that you use your gift of empathy, or the ability to understand how another person is feeling. If you have not understood the speaker's feelings, be patient and ask for more information.

---

### EXAMPLES

Linda asks, "Are you worried about Samantha's health?"

Dan says, "It sounds as if you're frightened of the risks associated with immunizations."

Mary states, "I can hear the frustration in your voice."

---

## DO NOT TALK! DO NOT TALK WHILE YOU ARE LISTENING

This is the Golden Rule of effective listening. Do not give advice. Do not tell something about yourself. Do not tell about another person's experience. Do not explain why the speaker misunderstands the situation. Do not tell the speaker why she should feel differently.

Think before you respond. Avoid automatic reactions that might be too hostile, defensive, or passive. Sometimes people don't want advice—they just want somebody to listen.

"It's a biological fact! No one can talk and listen at the same time."

## TAKE TIME TO THINK OVER YOUR RESPONSE

Don't feel rushed. If you feel confused, take a minute, a night, or a week to think about your response. For example, it is difficult to listen to criticism or bad news. It is very assertive to ask for some time to think things over before you give your response.

> **EXAMPLES**
>
> "This is strong feedback, and I don't know how to respond to your comments right now. I want to sleep on it. Let's talk again tomorrow."
> "I need some time to think this over. I'll call you back later."

## YOU CAN LISTEN RESPECTFULLY TO CRITICISM WITHOUT AGREEING WITH IT

The assertive truth is that you cannot please everybody all of the time. If you feel that the criticism is unfair, you can say so calmly. If the criticism seems fair, you can ask for some time to mull it over. Apologies are assertive, if you really believe you were at fault. If your pattern is to react to criticism passively, think over the situation before you apologize. Sometimes you must agree to disagree.

> **EXAMPLES**
>
> "I can see how you'd feel that way. I look at it from a different point of view."
> "I value your feedback, so thanks for sharing your opinions and suggestions with me. I know that's not always easy. Here's what I can do to help you."
> "You sound frustrated by my price increase, and I know your budget is already tight. I want to earn a better wage for my work with children. If you really can't live with that, then I agree that you must look for another provider."

## IT IS RESPECTFUL TO ASK PERMISSION TO GIVE FEEDBACK

Do not give a response until the speaker signals that he is ready to listen. Then you can ask for permission to give feedback or advice or to tell your own experiences.

---

**EXAMPLES**

"Do you want to hear what I think about this?"
"Can I tell you my opinion?"
"Would you like advice?"
"Do you want to hear about another parent who had a similar predicament?"

---

## DETACH YOURSELF EMOTIONALLY FROM AN ANGRY SPEAKER

When someone is angry at you, it does not mean you have to get angry, too. Try to be objective. Use empathy to understand the concern being voiced. Try to learn how the speaker came to his conclusions.

When you respond to an angry speaker, use a low, moderated voice. State facts and feelings honestly and clearly. Do not call names or throw insults. Behave professionally.

---

**EXAMPLES**

"You are very upset. I want to know more about this. Go on . . ."
"That must have been frightening for you! I'd be mad, too."
"Oh."

---

"Angry parents may have a laundry list of issues, and the most recent problem is the 'last straw.' You must listen to all the information to understand what angers them: is it simply the rate increase? Or is it the lost sock <u>plus</u> the day nobody said "hello" <u>plus</u> the unannounced substitute last week <u>PLUS</u> the rate increase?"

## EXAMPLES

A parent accused home provider Erik Frank of being greedy when he instituted his annual rate increase. From this situation Erik learned that his new business practice is relatively rare in his community. He learned that his policy statement was too long, and his customers weren't taking the time to read the details. Finally, he understood that his customers don't realize the business expenses that he must pay.

Any of these insights can help Erik to understand and improve his business. He might rewrite his policy statement, making it shorter and highlighting important points. He could write a letter to parents before he institutes his annual rate increase, to describe in general his increased business expenses. Erik could recognize his abilities as an innovative business manager and decide to mentor some new providers.

"Every criticism, no matter how unfair or impolite, gives you information about yourself. Ask yourself what you can learn from this criticism that might be helpful in the future."

# Role-Play

"Your child care children are learning valuable communication skills from your good example!"

Read through the following scenarios, and act out solutions to these real-life problems.

✔ Mr. and Mrs. Chinikaylo are angry when they hear that you will be increasing your rates for infant care. It is 5 p.m. Parents are arriving to pick up tired children. The Chinikaylo's are beginning to raise their voices, and they are obviously very upset by the prospective increase in the cost of their baby's full-time care. Although this family has been using child care for only two months, caring for their baby has been a comfortable transition for everyone and you would not like to lose their business. Your recent market rate survey convinced you that your infant care rate was too low for the market. Work to resolve this conflict with compassion and assertiveness.

✔ Mrs. Busch dropped off a lethargic, runny-nosed four-year-old son at child care today. When the little boy felt hot to your touch, you took his temperature and found that he was running a fever of 102 degrees. Your Sick Child Exclusion Policy states clearly that a child with a fever has a communicable disease and should not be in child care. When you phoned Mrs. Busch at work, she snapped, "I have a real job here! Finance is waiting for my report on the Big Top Investment Portfolio. I can't be bothered with this!" You are seething. Work to resolve this conflict with compassion and assertiveness.

✔ Your neighbor Bettina has been bringing her seven-year-old daughter Katie to part-time afternoon care for the past six months. Katie frequently returns to your child care facility after Bettina has picked her up, to continue playing with the other children in your care. You do not feel comfortable assuming responsibility for Katie's safety when you are not being paid to do so, and the girl's presence sometimes puts you over your numbers for registration. Bettina has a quick temper, and in the past she has made snide remarks about the inconvenience of having a child care business in the neighborhood. You feel that it is time to clear the air. Work to resolve this conflict with compassion and assertiveness.

# CHAPTER

# 8

## BUSINESS LESSON

# Cash In, Cash Out—
# Where Do You Stand?

## CREATE A CASH FLOW PLAN FOR YOUR BUSINESS

A **cash flow projection** gives you a lot of information about your business. For example, it can tell you the amount of unbudgeted funds available for unexpected expenses or facility improvements. It can project the amount of profit a provider can expect monthly or at year's end. It can remind you of the times of year that large periodic expenses like your annual **liability insurance** premium will be due, and it can assure you that the necessary funds will be available.

Here are the four easy steps you will need to follow to track your cash flow effectively and keep your business on course.

1. Draft a cash flow plan—a spreadsheet that projects your business income and expenses over a long period of time.

2. Project realistic numbers for expenses and income, as indicated by your ledger.

3. List income and expenses for every month, beginning with the profit or debt carried forward from the previous month.

4. At the end of the month, update your projection by listing your *real* income and expenses and calculating your *real* profit margin. Compare this to your projection and make any necessary corrections to your spending.

### Cash Flow Plan Exercise: Running Horse Child Care

Celia Running Horse was sure she had thought of everything when she submitted her loan application to First Bank for funding to start

> **Note!**
>
> When you predict earnings and expenses accurately, you can make intelligent financial decisions that keep your business profitable.

*Cash Flow Projection:* An estimate of income and expenses for a specific period of time in the future (usually one year). Shows the pattern of money coming into and going out of the business, indicating how much, and when, cash will be needed for operation of the business.

*Liability Insurance:* An insurance policy purchased by a child care business owner to protect him or her from being held liable for injuries, illnesses, deaths, or sexual molestation alleged to have resulted from child care.

"At first the cash flow plan spreadsheet looked intimidating. But when I started plugging in the income and expense figures from my record-keeping system, I realized that it was just simple addition and subtraction! My next goal is to put it on my computer."

a child care group home, Running Horse Child Care. Running Horse Child Care will be licensed for 2 adults to care for up to 12 children, in Celia's home. After receiving a loan of $2,000 ($1,500 to fence her yard and $500 to purchase two major pieces of child care equipment,) Celia has realized that she did not include in her loan request the $500 she needs to build playground equipment.

Now Celia has to decide whether to go back to the bank for the additional funding. She thinks that perhaps she can wait three months and earn enough profit to purchase the materials to build the playground equipment. That way it would be ready for use in late April. She uses a cash flow projection to make her decision.

Look at Celia's cash flow worksheet for January through March. The accompanying key contains the information you need to examine Celia's financial options. Read it carefully, as it explains several new terms and formulas that you will be using to chart your own business's cash flow. Definitions of new terminology are also provided in the Glossary. If Celia used her home computer, she could do all her calculations on a simple spreadsheet program.

# Key to Running Horse Child Care Cash Flow

## REVENUE

Revenue is all the monthly income received by Running Horse Child Care. Celia's goal, of course, is to maximize **total revenue** every month.

**Revenue:** Income received by business.

*Tuition*    Celia is confident that during the month of January she will fill eight of her 12 full-time slots at $420/month/child. In February, Celia plans to care for 10 full-time children. In March, one child's family will be taking a two-week vacation. Celia's contract states that each family is allowed two weeks of unpaid vacancy each year. The payment from that family will be reduced by 50 percent during March, to only $210.

*Food Program*    Celia will receive USDA Child and Adult Care Food Program reimbursement equal to $80/child. In January, she will receive $640; in February she will receive $800; in March, with the absence of one child for two weeks, her CACFP payment will be diminished by $40, to $760.

## DIRECT COSTS

Direct costs are the expenses that vary according to the number of children served. They are also known as variable expenses.

**Direct Costs:** Expenses that vary with numbers of customers served. Also known as *variable costs*, or in other industries, *cost of goods sold (COGS)*.

**Indirect Costs:** Expenses which do not vary with numbers of customers served. For a child care business, these include occupancy, utilities, telephone, training fees, printing. Also known as *fixed costs, operating costs,* or *overhead.*

*Labor*    In a child care business, **labor costs** include only the wages of care givers. (The wages of other staff, like cooks or maintenance workers, are considered **indirect costs**.) Celia pays herself $1,800/month, $1,500 to meet her living expenses and $300 to be set aside in a personal savings program. Her aide will earn $1,240/month. Celia's salary and the salary of her aide are $3,040/month.

*Substitute Provider*    Celia will also pay a substitute $50 to work at Running Horse Child Care while she attends a full-day training in February.

*Food*    Food costs will be $600 for January, $750 for February, and $670 for March.

*Other*    For one week in March, Celia has agreed to provide transportation from school. It will cost her .30/mile for four miles for five days, or a total of $6.

# Child Care Cash Flow Worksheet

Business Name: Running Horse
For Year: 2XXX

| Month of: | January | February | March | Total |
|---|---|---|---|---|
| **Slots filled:** | 8 | 10 | 10 | |
| Revenue | | | | |
| Child Care Tuition | $ 3,360 | $ 4,200 | $ 3,990 | $11,550 |
| Food Program Reimbursement | 640 | 800 | 760 | 2,200 |
| Other | | | | |
| TOTAL REVENUE | 4,000 | 5,000 | 4,750 | 13,750 |
| Direct Costs | | | | |
| Labor/Employment Taxes | 3,040 | 3,040 | 3,040 | 9,120 |
| Substitute Provider | | 50 | | 50 |
| Food | 600 | 750 | 670 | 2,020 |
| Other | | | 6 | 6 |
| TOTAL DIRECT COSTS | 3,640 | 3,840 | 3,716 | 11,196 |
| Direct Cost Percentage | 91% | 77% | 78% | 81% |
| Gross Profits | | | | |
| Gross Profit Percentage | 9% | 23% | 22% | 19% |
| Operating Costs | | | | |
| Advertising | 20 | | | 20 |
| Bank Fees | 10 | 10 | 10 | 30 |
| Child Care Supplies | 50 | 25 | 25 | 100 |
| Dues/Subscriptions | 35 | | | 35 |
| Insurance | | | 368 | 368 |
| Maintenance/Repairs | 25 | 50 | 50 | 125 |
| Mileage | | | | |
| Miscellaneous | 25 | 25 | 25 | 75 |
| Office Supplies | 20 | | | 20 |
| Postage | | | | |
| Printing | | | | |

# Child Care Cash Flow Worksheet (Continued)

**Business Name:** Running Horse
**For Year:** 2XXX

| Month of: | January | February | March | Total |
|---|---|---|---|---|
| Professional Fees | | 60 | | 60 |
| Rent | | | | |
| Taxes/Licenses for Business | 25 | | | 25 |
| Telephone | 15 | 15 | 15 | 45 |
| Travel | | | | |
| Training | | 10 | | 10 |
| Utilities | 130 | 130 | 130 | 390 |
| Wages/Administration | | | | |
| TOTAL OPERATING COSTS | 35 | 325 | 623 | 1,303 |
| NET PROFIT | 5 | 835 | 411 | 1,251 |
| Net Profit Percentage | 0% | 17% | 9% | 9% |
| Beginning Cash | $0 | $5 | $540 | |
| PLUS: | | | | |
| Net Profit | 5 | 835 | 411 | 1,251 |
| Loan Proceeds | 2,000 | | | 2,000 |
| Equity Injection | | | | |
| Grants Received | | | | |
| Donations | | | | |
| SUBTOTAL | 2,005 | 835 | 411 | 3,251 |
| MINUS: | | | | |
| Debt Service (Principle + Interest) | | 300 | 300 | 600 |
| Capital Expenditure | 1,500 | | | 1,500 |
| Major Equipment Purchase | 500 | | | 500 |
| Income Tax | | | | |
| Owner Draw | | | | |
| SUBTOTAL | 2,000 | 300 | 300 | 2,600 |
| Surplus <Deficit> | 5 | 535 | 111 | 651 |
| Ending Cash | $5 | $540 | $651 | |

*Direct Cost Percentage:*
The percentage of child care provider's income that goes into business expenses directly related to caring for children.

*Gross Profit:* Total revenue minus direct costs. Also known as *gross profit margin.*

*Gross Profit Percentage:* Gross profit divided by total revenue, times 100. The percentage of total revenue left after cost of goods sold.

*Operating Costs:* Expenses that do not vary with numbers of customers served. For a child care business, these include occupancy, utilities, telephone, training fees, printing. Also known as *fixed costs, indirect costs,* or *overhead.*

*Direct Cost Percentage*    The **direct cost percentage** is the percentage of Celia's income that goes into business expenses directly related to caring for children. To calculate it, divide the total direct costs by total revenue and multiply by 100.

## GROSS PROFIT

Determine Celia's **gross profit** for each month by subtracting her monthly expenses from her monthly total income.

*Gross Profit Percentage*    The **gross profit percentage** is the percentage of Celia's income that remains after she pays direct costs. To calculate it, divide gross profit by total revenue and multiply by 100.

## OPERATING COSTS

**Operating costs** are the expenses that don't vary with the number of children served. They are also known as fixed costs, indirect costs, or overhead.

*Advertising*    This is one of several start-up costs that Celia will pay in January. She will advertise in the local newspaper to fill her vacant slots, and the ad will cost her $20.

*Bank Fees*    Celia will pay $10/month for a banking service fee.

*Child Care Supplies/Materials*    Celia has allocated $50 in January, $25 in February, and $25 in March for child care supplies and materials.

*Dues/Subscriptions*    Celia will pay $35 in January to join her local Family Child Care Association.

*Insurance*    Celia's annual bill for her child care liability and fire insurance policy will be due in March.

*Maintenance/Repair*    Celia has allocated $25 in January, $50 in February, and $50 in March for repair and maintenance of her child care rooms.

*Miscellaneous*    Just to be on the safe side, Celia has set aside $25/month for miscellaneous expenses.

*Office Supplies*    As another start-up cost, Celia will spend $20 in January on office supplies.

*Professional Services*    In February, Celia will pay an accountant $60 to prepare her tax return.

*Taxes/Licenses*    Celia must purchase a municipal business license in January for $25.

*Telephone*    Celia has budgeted $15/month for necessary long distance calls to the Department of Family Services, which she will make on her home telephone service.

*Training*    Celia plans to attend a full-day training at the local CCR&R in February.

*Utilities*    Celia will pay $130/month this winter for gas heat and electricity for her child-care rooms.

## NET PROFIT

Total Celia's expenses for each month from January to March. Subtract these amounts from monthly gross profit to determine monthly **net profit**.

*Net Profit Percentage*    The **net profit percentage** tells you the percentage of Celia's revenue that remains after all expenses have been paid. To calculate it, divide net profit by total revenue, then multiply by 100.

*Net Profit:* Total revenue minus direct costs and operating costs. Also known as *net profit margin.*

*Net Profit Percentage:* Net profit divided by total revenue, times 100. The percentage of total revenue left after all expenses.

## PLUS AND LESS

At the bottom of the spreadsheet, you will see a section headed *PLUS* and a section headed *LESS*. This is where you chart the ins and outs of Celia's cash. Assume that all parents' payments are received by the tenth of each month.

*Beginning Cash*    Celia starts in January with a **beginning cash** balance of $0. Each month's beginning cash is carried over from the **ending cash** balance of the previous month.

*Beginning Cash:* Total cash in checking account, savings, and petty cash fund at the beginning of any accounting period.

*Ending Cash:* Total cash in checking account, savings, and petty cash fund at the end of any accounting period.

## PLUS

To each month's beginning cash, Celia adds the child-care income remaining after expenses and any other additional income that she may have received.

*Net Profit*    This is the amount of revenue that remains after Celia pays all of her expenses.

*Loan Proceeds*    The total amount of Celia's loan, $2,000, is received in one lump sum in January.

*Loan Proceeds:* The amount of money disbursed by a lender to a borrower.

**Equity Injection:** The value of items or money contributed by the owner for use by the business.

**Debt Service:** Money spent to repay debt, including both principle and interest.

**Capital Expenditure:** The amount spent for any asset or improvement that will be used in a business for more than one year.

**Major Equipment Expense:** Funds spent for the purchase of equipment typically valued over $100 and used in the business for more than one year. These items can generally be depreciated.

**Time/Space Percentage:** A formula determining which portion of a home is used for business purposes and the financial value of that use. Used in calculating the percentage of a home child care provider's home expenses that can be deducted as business expenses for tax purposes.

**Owner Draw:** Money taken from profits of a business for the personal use of the owner.

**Surplus:** An amount in excess of a certain number.

**Deficit:** A shortage in funds. Your checking account has a deficit when your balance is negative or "in the red."

*Equity Injection*    **Equity injection** is the term used to describe the value of items or money contributed by the owner for use by the business. Celia does not plan to add any of her personal savings to the business this winter.

*Grants Received*    Celia has not applied for any grants this year.

*Donations*    Celia will not seek donations this year.

*Other*    Celia anticipates no other income this year.

## LESS

After totaling the PLUS column, Celia subtracts any of the following expenses that might apply to her business.

*Debt Service (Principle and Interest)*    Celia will repay her loan at $300/month, beginning in February.

*Capital Expenditure*    This is the $1,500 cost of the new fence.

*Major Equipment Expense*    This is the $500 cost of two major pieces of child care equipment.

*Income Tax*    Celia is certain that if she keeps good records of her business expenses, including the **time/space percentage** of household expenses her accountant has helped her calculate, she will have enough deductions that she will not owe any income taxes this year.

*Owner Draw*    The **owner draw** is the amount of profit that a business owner takes for her personal use. Celia isn't budgeting to take any right now, although she hopes that next year's budget allows a monthly draw.

## SURPLUS OR DEFICIT

Celia subtracts the LESS subtotal from the PLUS subtotal for each month. The answer tells her whether she made or lost money, determined by whether she has a **surplus** or a **deficit**.

## ENDING CASH

Celia adds the month's final surplus or deficit to the beginning cash balance to calculate how much money she has in the bank at the end of each month.

## Answer these questions for Celia:

- ✔ How much cash is left in the business at the end of each month?

- ✔ At the end of the third month, will there be enough cash to purchase materials to build the playground equipment?

- ✔ Assuming that her costs don't change from January to March, should Celia plan to purchase the playground equipment at the end of March? Why or why not?

- ✔ What kinds of things could happen that would change Celia's cash flow projection?

- ✔ If Celia decides she cannot afford to purchase the playground equipment at the end of March, what could she do differently from January through March to make this purchase possible? She absolutely does not want to go back to the bank for another loan.

- ✔ Has Celia forgotten anything in this cash flow plan?

## DRAFT AN ANNUAL INCOME STATEMENT

At the end of the year, you will want to know how much money your business actually made. To do this, businesses take information from their monthly ledgers and apply it to an **income statement.** Here's an example from provider Samaya Yafai for her business, Rainbow Home Child Care. The accompanying key explains the terms that you will use to assess your year-end income. Definitions are also provided in the Glossary.

*Income Statement:* A document showing the sources and amount of income; the costs and expenses of providing service; and the amount of resulting profit (or loss) during a specific time period. Also known as a *profit and loss statement.*

# Rainbow Home Child Care

## Samaya Yafai, Owner

## Income Statement

For period from **January 1**, 2XXX to **December 31**, 2XXX

| | |
|---|---:|
| Child Care Revenue (Tuition, USDA Food Program, Interest) . . . . . . . . . . . . . . | **$27,840** |
| Minus Direct Costs (Includes provider wages) . . . . . . . . . . . . . . . . . . . . . . . | **-18,000** |
| Gross Profit . . . . . . . . . . . . . . . . . . . . . . . . . . . . . . . . . . . . . . . . . . . . . . . | **. 9,840** |
| Minus Operating Costs . . . . . . . . . . . . . . . . . . . . . . . . . . . . . . . . . . . . . . . . | **- 5,880** |
| Net Profit . . . . . . . . . . . . . . . . . . . . . . . . . . . . . . . . . . . . . . . . . . . . . . . . . | **$ 3,960** |
| Minus Capital Expenditures . . . . . . . . . . . . . . . . . . . . . . . . . . . . . . . . . . . . . | **- 0** |
| Minus Interest Expense . . . . . . . . . . . . . . . . . . . . . . . . . . . . . . . . . . . . . . . . | **- 600** |
| Minus Depreciation . . . . . . . . . . . . . . . . . . . . . . . . . . . . . . . . . . . . . . . . . . . | **- 300** |
| Income Before Taxes . . . . . . . . . . . . . . . . . . . . . . . . . . . . . . . . . . . . . . . . . | **$ 3,060** |
| Minus Income Tax Expenses . . . . . . . . . . . . . . . . . . . . . . . . . . . . . . . . . . . . | **- 505** |
| Net Income . . . . . . . . . . . . . . . . . . . . . . . . . . . . . . . . . . . . . . . . . . . . . . . . | **$ 2,555** |

# Key to Rainbow Home Child Care Income Statement

Use the following key to understand how Samaya Yafai completed her statement.

## CHILD CARE REVENUE

This is Samaya's total income for the year.

## DIRECT COSTS

These are costs that depend on the numbers of children served (for example, food and provider wages).

## GROSS PROFIT

Revenue minus direct costs equals gross profit.

## OPERATING COSTS

These are the fixed expenses that are incurred regardless of numbers of children served (for example, phone and utilities).

## NET PROFIT

Revenue minus direct and operating costs equals net profit.

## INTEREST EXPENSE

Samaya's loan payment to Montana Community Development Corporation includes $50 per month interest.

*Interest Expense:* Interest paid on business loan or any other payable.

## DEPRECIATION

The diminishing value of Samaya's property and equipment, called **depreciation**, is calculated from a schedule prepared for Samaya by her CPA.

*Depreciation:* Annual reduction in value of land, buildings, equipment, or furniture according to IRS schedule.

## EARNINGS BEFORE TAXES

Net profit minus interest expense and depreciation equals earnings before taxes.

## INCOME TAX EXPENSES

**Income tax expenses** in this case are 15 percent of Samaya's earnings before taxes, as calculated by her CPA.

*Income Tax Expense:* Annual or quarterly federal, state, and local taxes.

## NET INCOME

**Net Income:** Total income remaining after all expenses are paid.

Earnings before taxes minus income tax expenses equals **net income**, or the total income remaining after all expenses are paid.

### Answer these questions for Samaya:

- ✔ Not counting Samaya's wages, did she make a profit this year? How much was it?
- ✔ What percentage of total revenue was Samaya's net income?
- ✔ Samaya didn't expect her business to profit this year. Name some ways she could use this money to strengthen her business.

## COMPLETE A BALANCE SHEET (STATEMENT OF ASSETS AND LIABILITIES)

**Balance Sheet:** A document that shows *business assets* (what the business owns) and *business liabilities* (what the business owes) at a specific date. Also shows *owner's equity* (owner's personal investment plus profits).

Complete a **balance sheet** at least once a year, to show the value of what is owned and what is owed by your business. A balance sheet provides a snapshot of the business at a specific moment in time. By comparing balance sheets kept over a period of time, a business owner can track growth in the value of her business. For an example, look at Samaya Yafai's balance sheet, drafted at the end of 1999.

# Rainbow Home Child Care—Samaya Yafai, Provider

## Balance Sheet

Statement of Assets and Liabilities as of **December 31**, 2XXX

| ASSETS | | LIABILITIES | |
|---|---|---|---|
| **Current Assets** | | **Current Liabilities** | |
| Cash | $1,200 | Accounts Payable | $ 25 |
| Accounts Receivable | 240 | Income Tax Payable | 505 |
| Inventory | 300 | Short-Term Loan Payable | 0 |
| Prepaid Expenses | 360 | Current Portion, Long-Term | 190 |
| Total Current Assets | $2,100 | Total Current Liabilities | $ 720 |
| **Fixed Assets** | | **Long-Term Liabilities** | |
| Land, Building, Equipment, and Furniture | $2,000 | Long-Term Loan Payable | $ 760 |
| Less Depreciation | -300 | Other | 0 |
| Total Fixed Assets | $1,700 | Total Long-Term Liabilities | $ 760 |
| **Total Current Assets** | $2,100 | **Total Current Liabilities** | $ 720 |
| <u>**Total Fixed Assets**</u> | +1,700 | <u>**Total Long-Term Liabilities**</u> | + 760 |
| **TOTAL ASSETS** | $3,800 | **TOTAL LIABILITIES** | $1,480 |
| | | **OWNER'S EQUITY** | +$2,320 |
| TOTAL ASSETS | $3,800 | TOTAL LIABILITIES + OWNER'S EQUITY | $3,800 |

"Total liabilities plus owner's equity equals (or <u>balances</u>) total assets. Get it?"

# Key to Rainbow Home Child Care Balance Sheet

Use the following key to understand how Samaya Yafai completed her balance sheet.

## CURRENT ASSETS

*Cash*    On December 31, at the end of her fiscal year, Samaya has $1,200 in the bank.

*Accounts Receivable*    One parent owes Samaya $240, so she has **accounts receivable** in this amount.

*Inventory*    Samaya has $300 worth of arts and crafts supplies on hand, representing her **inventory**.

*Prepaid Expenses*    Samaya has prepaid her 2000 business liability insurance.

*Total Current Assets*    Samaya totals the four items listed above.

*Accounts Receivable:* Money owed to the business.

*Inventory:* Dollar value of consumable supplies and materials on hand.

## FIXED ASSETS

*Land, Building, Equipment, and Furniture*    Samaya owns no land or buildings, but she has $2,000 worth of child care equipment and furniture.

*Depreciation*    This is the diminishing value of Samaya's property and equipment, according to a **depreciation schedule** provided by Samaya's CPA.

*Total Fixed Assets*    Value of land, building, equipment and furniture minus depreciation equals total fixed assets.

*Depreciation Schedule:* A table showing the amount per year and number of years over which an asset is depreciated.

## TOTAL ASSETS

Total current assets plus fixed assets equals total assets.

## CURRENT LIABILITIES

*Accounts Payable*    Samaya owes the printer $25 for her new business cards; this is her **accounts payable** total.

*Income Tax Payable*    Samaya is projecting that she will owe 15 percent of earnings before taxes.

*Short-Term Loan Payable*    Samaya does not have a short-term loan.

*Accounts Payable:* Bills to be paid.

*Current Portion, Long-Term Loan Payable*   Samaya will pay $190 this year toward her business loan.

*Total Current Liabilities*   Samaya totals the four items listed here as total current **liabilities**.

*Liabilities:* Value of everything owed by the business, including accounts payable, income taxes, and loan payments. A *current liability* is a debt that will be payed within the current year; a *long-term liability* is a debt that will be carried for longer than the current year.

## LONG-TERM LIABILITIES

*Long-Term Loan Payable*   After this year, Samaya still owes $760 on her loan.

*Other*   This category could include mortgage payment, vehicle loan, or any expense paid over a period lasting longer than one year.

## TOTAL LIABILITIES

Total current liabilities plus long-term liabilities equals total liabilities.

## OWNER'S EQUITY

Total assets minus total liabilities, equals the net worth of Samaya's business on December 31, 2XXX. This is the amount of **equity** she has in her business.

*Equity:* That portion of the total value of the business that is equal to the owner's investment plus profit.

## SPREADSHEET SOFTWARE PROGRAMS

Use one of the computer software programs to create simple spreadsheets that do your addition, subtraction, and percentages in these spreadsheets. These programs include Lotus 1-2-3, Quattro Pro, and Excel.

You could purchase a pre-programmed diskette designed to accompany this curriculum, including instructions and spreadsheets for break-even analysis, cash flow plan, income statement, and balance sheet. Order from the Montana Child Care Resource & Referral Network by using the order form at the back of this book.

"Now I can see the value of my business growing year by year. When I am ready to retire, I'll be able to sell my business. Meanwhile, I know I have my expenses covered, and I'm even saving for a Caribbean vacation!"

"Now you're really getting a handle on the true value of your child care business."

✔ Using the Cash Flow Worksheet at the end of this chapter, complete a cash flow plan for your business, projecting income and expenses for the next 6 to 12 months.

✔ Write one brief paragraph describing your income for the next 12 months. Will your business have adequate cash flow to cover all expenses and to meet your profit goals?

✔ Using the Income Statement Worksheet at the end of this chapter, complete an annual income statement for your business. (If you do not have complete financial records now, do this at the end of the year.)

✔ Using the Balance Sheet Worksheet at the end of this chapter, complete a balance sheet for your business. (If you do not have complete finanical records now, do this at the end of the year.

✔ Write one brief paragraph describing your business' **profitability.** Is it profitable, breaking even, or losing money? Why is it in this position?

*Profitability:* The ability of a business to make a profit, break even, or lose profit.

# Child Care Cash Flow Projection

**Business Name:**
**For Year Of:**

| Month: | Jan | Feb | Mar | Apr | May | June | July | Aug | Sep | Oct | Nov | Dec | Total |
|---|---|---|---|---|---|---|---|---|---|---|---|---|---|
| **Slots filled:** | | | | | | | | | | | | | |
| Revenue | | | | | | | | | | | | | |
| Tuition | | | | | | | | | | | | | |
| USDA | | | | | | | | | | | | | |
| Other | | | | | | | | | | | | | |
| TOTAL | | | | | | | | | | | | | |
| Direct Costs | | | | | | | | | | | | | |
| Labor/ Employment Taxes | | | | | | | | | | | | | |
| Substitute | | | | | | | | | | | | | |
| Food | | | | | | | | | | | | | |
| Other | | | | | | | | | | | | | |
| TOTAL | | | | | | | | | | | | | |
| Direct Cost % | | | | | | | | | | | | | |
| GROSS PROFIT | | | | | | | | | | | | | |
| Gross Profit % | | | | | | | | | | | | | |
| Operating Costs | | | | | | | | | | | | | |
| Advertising | | | | | | | | | | | | | |
| Bank Fees | | | | | | | | | | | | | |
| Child Care Supplies | | | | | | | | | | | | | |
| Dues/ Subscriptions | | | | | | | | | | | | | |
| Insurance | | | | | | | | | | | | | |
| Maintenance/ Repair | | | | | | | | | | | | | |
| Mileage | | | | | | | | | | | | | |
| Miscellaneous | | | | | | | | | | | | | |
| Office Supplies | | | | | | | | | | | | | |
| Payroll Taxes | | | | | | | | | | | | | |
| Postage | | | | | | | | | | | | | |
| Printing | | | | | | | | | | | | | |

# Child Care Cash Flow Projection (Continued)

**Business Name:**
**For Year Of:**

| Month: | Jan | Feb | Mar | Apr | May | June | July | Aug | Sep | Oct | Nov | Dec | Total |
|---|---|---|---|---|---|---|---|---|---|---|---|---|---|
| Professional Services | | | | | | | | | | | | | |
| Rent | | | | | | | | | | | | | |
| Taxes/Licenses | | | | | | | | | | | | | |
| Telephone | | | | | | | | | | | | | |
| Travel | | | | | | | | | | | | | |
| Training | | | | | | | | | | | | | |
| Utilities | | | | | | | | | | | | | |
| Wages/ Administration | | | | | | | | | | | | | |
| TOTAL | | | | | | | | | | | | | |
| NET PROFIT | | | | | | | | | | | | | |
| Net Profit % | | | | | | | | | | | | | |
| Beginning Cash | | | | | | | | | | | | | |
| PLUS: | | | | | | | | | | | | | |
| Net Profit | | | | | | | | | | | | | |
| Loan Proceeds | | | | | | | | | | | | | |
| Equity Injection | | | | | | | | | | | | | |
| Grants Received | | | | | | | | | | | | | |
| Donations | | | | | | | | | | | | | |
| Other | | | | | | | | | | | | | |
| SUBTOTAL | | | | | | | | | | | | | |
| LESS: | | | | | | | | | | | | | |
| Debt Service (P & I) | | | | | | | | | | | | | |
| Capital Expenditure | | | | | | | | | | | | | |
| Major Equipment | | | | | | | | | | | | | |
| Income Tax | | | | | | | | | | | | | |
| Owner Draw | | | | | | | | | | | | | |
| SUBTOTAL | | | | | | | | | | | | | |
| Surplus <Deficit> | | | | | | | | | | | | | |
| Ending Cash | | | | | | | | | | | | | |

# Income Statement

**Name of Program:**

**For period from** _____ , 20__ to ___ , 20__

Child Care Revenue . . . . . . . . . . . . . . . . . . . . . . . . . . . . . . . . $ _____

Minus Direct Costs . . . . . . . . . . . . . . . . . . . . . . . . . . . . . . . − _____

Equals Gross Profit . . . . . . . . . . . . . . . . . . . . . . . . . . . . . . . = _____


Gross Profit . . . . . . . . . . . . . . . . . . . . . . . . . . . . . . . . . . . $ _____

Minus Operating Costs . . . . . . . . . . . . . . . . . . . . . . . . . . . − _____

Equals Net Profit . . . . . . . . . . . . . . . . . . . . . . . . . . . . . . . = _____


Net Profit . . . . . . . . . . . . . . . . . . . . . . . . . . . . . . . . . . . . $ _____

Minus Capital Expenditures . . . . . . . . . . . . . . . . . . . . . . . − _____

Minus Interest Expense . . . . . . . . . . . . . . . . . . . . . . . . . . − _____

Minus Depreciation . . . . . . . . . . . . . . . . . . . . . . . . . . . . . − _____

Equals Income Before Taxes . . . . . . . . . . . . . . . . . . . . . . = _____


Income Before Taxes . . . . . . . . . . . . . . . . . . . . . . . . . . . . $ _____

Minus Income Tax Expenses . . . . . . . . . . . . . . . . . . . . . . − _____

Equals Net Income . . . . . . . . . . . . . . . . . . . . . . . . . . . . . = _____

# Balance Sheet

Statement of Assets and Liabilities as of _____, 20___

**Program Name:**

| **ASSETS** | **LIABILITIES** |
|---|---|
| **Current Assets** | **Current Liabilities** |
| Cash . . . . . . . . . . . . . . . . . $ _____ | Accounts Payable . . . . . . . . $ _____ |
| Accounts Receivable . . . . . . . + _____ | Income Tax Payable . . . . . . + _____ |
| Inventory . . . . . . . . . . . . . . + _____ | Short-Term Loan Payable . . + _____ |
| Prepaid Expenses . . . . . . . . + _____ | Current Portion, Long-Term + _____ |
| Total Current Assets . . . . . . . $ _____ | Total Current Liabilities . . . . $ _____ |
| **Fixed Assets** | **Long-Term Liabilities** |
| Land, Building, Equipment, and Furniture . . . . . . . . . . . $ _____ | Long-Term Loan Payable . . $ _____ |
| Less Depreciation . . . . . . . . − _____ | Other . . . . . . . . . . . . . . . . + _____ |
| Total Fixed Assets . . . . . . . . $ _____ | Total Long-Term Liabilities  $ _____ |
| **Total Current Assets** . . . . . $ _____ | **Total Current Liabilities**  $ _____ |
| **Total Fixed Assets** . . . . . . . + _____ | **Total Long-Term Liabilities**  + _____ |
| **TOTAL ASSETS** . . . . . . . . $ _____ | **TOTAL LIABILITIES** . . . . $ _____ |
| | **OWNER'S EQUITY** . . . . . . $ _____ |
| TOTAL ASSETS . . . . . . . . . . $ _____ = | TOTAL LIABILITIES + OWNER'S EQUITY . . . . . . . $ _____ |

# 9

## COMMUNICATION LESSON

# Sharing Unpleasant Information with Parents

Eventually, and inevitably, a business owner will have to tell somebody something that he does not want to hear. This may happen when a provider turns away a prospective customer, raises a concern about a child's health or safety out of the child care environment, or changes her payment policies.

At these times a provider will find it helpful to remember her rights as a professional, fight the tendency to react with guilt, and admit that it is no fun to deliver bad news! Read through this checklist for a reminder of the traits of assertive communication.

> **Note!**
>
> Learn to share unpleasant or critical information in a respectful, supportive manner.

## ASSERTIVENESS CHECKLIST FOR SHARING UNPLEASANT INFORMATION

Keep these traits in mind:

- ✔ I am not looking for a winner and loser in this encounter.
- ✔ I respect the rights, opinions, and feelings of others.
- ✔ I choose an appropriate time for this discussion, to give my listener a chance to ask for clarification and share thoughts and feelings with me.
- ✔ I encourage negotiation and compromise to find a solution.
- ✔ I look creatively for a solution acceptable to both parties.
- ✔ I express clearly the limits of my flexibility.
- ✔ I listen carefully for the limits of the other party's flexibility.

# GIVING CONSTRUCTIVE CRITICISM

There will be times when you need to talk to a parent about their behavior that causes a problem for your business. To maintain good relations between provider and parent, you must give this information in a constructive, supportive manner. Here is a formula that will help you practice what you want to say. Just remember the key word, B-E-A-D.

## "B" Is for Behavior

The speaker describes the specific *behavior* that is causing the problem. Your point of view must be objective and rational. In other words, show no feelings here.

## "E" Is for Emotion

Now it is time for you to share your *emotions*. Use a calm voice, and share the feelings that this behavior generates in you. Do not make the mistake of telling your thoughts—use feeling words (for example, "worried", "hurt", "unappreciated", "frustrated", "frightened").

Anger is a feeling, but usually another feeling is underlying as well. When you express anger, identify and share the "root" feeling.

## "A" Is for Alternatives

Suggest several *alternatives* that would be acceptable to you, and emphasize clearly which one would make you happiest. You may have to think about this before you are ready to talk. Offer a range of alternatives, if possible. Ask for suggestions. This step demonstrates your willingness to find a solution that benefits both parties and to compromise if you can.

## "D" Is for Decision

Tell your *decision*, your choice among the alternatives you have generated. This may be a compromise or a consequence. State your bottom line, telling the positive outcome that you believe this change will bring.

# Role-Play

A parent at Sunrise Preschool has been consistently irresponsible in paying her child care bills. Preschool owner Lynn Lee's system is one of monthly payment on the first of the month, which Lynn believes is convenient for both customer and provider. Four of the past six months she has had to ask Mrs. Banks for her payment. Sunrise Preschool policies include a late payment fee, but Lynn has never charged it. Occasionally, other parents are late with payment, but none is ever as consistently late as Mrs. Banks.

Put yourself in Lynn Lee's place, and think of your own way to give Mrs. Banks the constructive criticism that the situation demands. Using the outline below, write down your ideas by following the B-E-A-D formula to organize your assertive response.

**"B" is for Behavior**

**"E" is for Emotion**

**"A" is for Alternatives**

**"D" is for Decision**

"I try to live by the '24-Hour Rule.' If something bothers me for longer than 24 hours, then I need to discuss it with the parent as soon as possible. To let it go on only makes things worse."

"These skills will help you to communicate more clearly with parents about your business practices. But there is a lot more to learn about provider/parent partnerships! Check out the resources in Appendix C."

# 10

## BUSINESS LESSON

# Marketing Strategies

A business owner must maintain a stable income. The healthiest child care businesses pay attention to how they market their service to keep slots as full as possible. We all know a lot about marketing. We see it every day in television commercials, radio advertising, newspaper and magazine ads. But marketing also includes the smaller day-to-day outreach activities of businesses: logos, business cards, telephone book listings, church bulletin announcements, telephone answering machine messages, word-of-mouth referrals, and vanity license plates! The "best practices" listed keep a child care business in the public eye. Think **marketing strategy**.

> **Note!**
>
> Research your local market, identify the special features of your business, target your best customers, and get your message out. And, remember—your message tells how your service meets your customers' needs!

## FOUR STEPS TO A MARKETING PLAN

Follow these steps to develop a marketing plan:

1. Define your service.
2. Define your market.
3. Develop specific strategies to reach your market.
4. Do it!

*Marketing Strategy:* A specific plan for attracting customers to a business.

## RESEARCH THE CHILD CARE INDUSTRY—NATIONALLY AND LOCALLY

Learn what is happening in the child care industry today, across the nation and in your town. To understand the current market trends, ask yourself these questions. What kind of child care supply and demand exists in your community? Is child care available for every family that wants it? What types of care are difficult for parents to find? Are there certain days and hours of care that are hard to find? Are there types of employment that make child care arrangements challenging? Are there types of care for which parents pay more in your community?

✎ _____

✎ _____

---

### EXAMPLE

The largest center serving the West Valley neighborhood just closed, reducing the availability of child care in that part of town. The CCR&R reports that demand for infant care outweighs supply, 2 to 1. Parents pay more for part-time care. Monthly prepayment is becoming popular with home child care businesses. During September and January, peak times of the year for child care changes, parents are forced to use informal child care arrangements.

---

## LEARN THE SIZE OF YOUR MARKET

Identify the geographic area from which your customer families come. What is the geographic area that you can expect to serve? What's happening to the population demographics of your community; for example, are numbers of young families growing?

✎ _____

✎ _____

Providers needing more information about their community's child care market can check with the local child care resource and referral agency, the neighborhood elementary school, Head Start, or the local child care provider association.

## ANALYZE THE COMPETITION

Know your competition and the market niches that they fill. **Competitors** are businesses or individuals who provide a similar service. There are two types: *direct competitors* and *indirect competitors.* Ask yourself these questions: Who are your direct competitors? Who are their customers, and what are the most popular services that they provide? Name and describe the most successful businesses. Name and describe the least successful businesses.

*Competitors:* A business or individual who provides a similar service. There are two types: *direct competitors* and *indirect competitors*. The direct competitors of a home-based child care business are other home-based child care businesses. The indirect competitors of a home-based child care business are all other types of child care available (centers, preschools, family members.)

**EXAMPLE**

In the East Pines and Hillview areas, there are eight family child care homes, one after-school program, and the Head Start preschool. All programs offer daytime care, five days a week. None offer weekend or evening services. All accept child care payment assistance vouchers. The after-school and Head Start programs are full, with waiting lists. The three most successful home programs have professional names, with signs and attractive outdoor play equipment in neat, fenced front yards.

## DESCRIBE YOUR CHILD CARE SERVICES

Identify the special features of your business that benefit your customers. List the customer benefits that your service offers (for example, part-time care schedules; locations near schools, business district, hospital, or a rural neighborhood; transportation to kindergarten or lessons; art and music curriculum; participation in child care payment assistance programs; professional certification).

"Why not keep a stack of these on hand to give to parents at their initial interview?"

Write a one- to two-line description of your business, highlighting your special features.

✎ _____

> **EXAMPLE**
>
> Manuela's Child Care Home offers flexible scheduling for weekday care. She cares for infants and toddlers in an intimate, home-like setting. Manuela has earned her Associate's degree in child development, has 10 years of experience caring for very young children, and participates in the Child and Adult Care Food Program.

## IDENTIFY YOUR COMPETITIVE EDGE

Describe the service you provide that is unique in your community. Try to define the features that make your business stand out from its competitors. List specific competitive qualities of your business. For example, do you offer a high adult-to-child ratio, an attractive facility and play area, convenient hours or location, high value at a reasonable cost, a home-like setting, sibling care, or non-traditional hours care?

✎ _____

> **EXAMPLE**
>
> Care Bear Child Care offers convenience to parents through flexible hours of care and an easy monthly billing system. Children's social and mental development are supported by a curriculum that emphasizes enjoyment of reading and cooperative play. Participation in the Child and Adult Care Food Program keeps parents' food costs down and guarantees on-site monitoring visits from a child development specialist three times per year.

## IDENTIFY YOUR CUSTOMERS

***Customer Profile:*** A description of a typical customer. Categories often used to describe the customer include age, income level, education, profession, geographic area, lifestyle, or interests.

Create a **customer profile**. Determine who uses your service, and describe these customers. List the traits that they have in common. Are they single-parent families, dual-career families, student parents? Do they work full time, part time, weekends, evenings? Are they parents of infants, preschoolers, school-agers, or all of the above? Where do they live and work? What do they like to do for fun? Write a one to two-sentence description of your customers.

✎ _____

## IDENTIFY YOUR TARGET MARKET

Create a preferred-customer profile. Who do you want your customers to be? Describe the families you want to serve. Ask yourself who needs the special features of your child care? Who lives or works near your business? How can these customers be reached?

✎ _____

✎ _____

✎ _____

> **EXAMPLE**
>
> My target market includes families living in Grant Creek or East City. Their work is located near home or downtown. Their children are infants to preschoolers. Parents work part-time shifts or have flexible schedules.

## BEGIN MARKETING NOW

Do not wait until you have vacancies to begin marketing! With ongoing marketing activities, a provider minimizes the likelihood of lengthy vacancies in her business. A marketing plan need not be elaborate or expensive. You can build the cost of marketing into your annual budget. And don't forget that marketing costs are a tax-deductible business expense.

"If you can not afford to advertise, you can not afford to be in business."

## DEVELOP A MARKETING CALENDAR

List the specific activities that you will do to market your business, month by month, in an annual time line or *marketing calendar*.

# Marketing Calendar

**August**

✔ Sign up for CCR&R referral list.

**September**

✔ Develop logo, business card, and advertising flyer. Emphasize flexible scheduling, monthly billing system, professional background, experience working with young children, intimacy of home environment, one-on-one attention to children, participation in the Child and Adult Care Food Program.

✔ Record professional-sounding answering machine message.

✔ Train family in telephone etiquette and message taking.

**October**

✔ Get magnetic business sign for my car doors.

✔ Get permission to post flyers in break rooms at Community Hospital Outpatient Surgical Center, Sunrise Sports, Fact and Fiction Bookstore, and Lucky Strike Casino & Restaurant.

**November**

✔ Make business sign for front fence.

✔ Move children's play area to fenced front yard.

**December**

✔ Seek permission to post business card on outside wall of Global Espresso Stand, at the corner of my street. In return, make quarterly advance purchase of complementary "Monday Morning Mocha" for customers. Parents can stop for free coffee drink on their way to work.

**February**

✔ Call Uptown Child Care Association to plan Worthy Wage Day activity.

# Marketing Calendar

## April

✔ Tape business card to Week of the Young Child flyers. Post at Mini-Mall, Neighborhood Laundromat.

## May

✔ Write letter to the editor re: Worthy Wage Day.

## Plan for Upcoming Vacancies

✔ Alert CCR&R referral service before vacancies occur.

✔ Run classified ad in Sunday *Daily Courier*.

✔ Post flyers at Neighborhood Laundromat and Easy Convenience Market.

## Ongoing Activities

✔ Encourage parents to tell friends about vacancies. Offer one day's free care to parent whose referral leads to a new customer.

✔ Use business cards always! Keep parents supplied with cards to distribute at work.

## TAKE AN OUTSIDER'S LOOK AT YOUR FACILITY

Be sure that a potential customer gets the right impression when he stands outside your facility or when he enters your business. Stand across the street from your business, then run down the following checklist.

- ✔ Does your facility look warm and inviting, professional and safe?
- ✔ Is the yard clean, with planted flower beds or simple landscaping?
- ✔ Is play equipment safe, clean, attractive, and appropriate to the age of the children you serve?
- ✔ Is your dog securely fenced in the back yard, away from the children's play areas?
- ✔ Are your business name and logo displayed on an exterior sign on the lawn or in your front window?

Walk in the door to your child care area, and look at it as if you are a parent seeing it for the first time. Ask yourself these questions.

- ✔ Is the interior clean, bright, and orderly?
- ✔ Is the interior set up for adults or children?
- ✔ Are there objects and activities at children's eye level?
- ✔ Is the space welcoming?
- ✔ Will your child want to stay there all day, or would you?

## PROJECT A PROFESSIONAL IMAGE

Choose a business name and logo that identify your professional image, appealing to the type of customer you want to serve, and use them on everything you make! Sketch some imaginative logos for your business, or clip examples from the newspaper or phone book. Visualize your logo on business cards, letterhead, a telephone book ad, and your exterior sign. Use your imagination to invent a few names for your child care business that are compatible with the market you serve.

 _____

## USE BUSINESS CARDS

Carry your business cards wherever you go. Hand them out anytime you discuss your work, your facility, or your customers. Post them in places where people have to sit for long waiting periods. Business cards are inexpensive, durable, bright, and attractive. List people to whom you could give your business card and places where you could post or display them.

✎ _____

✎ _____

## BEWARE OF BROCHURES

Consider your options carefully before you print an advertising brochure. A brochure can be expensive to develop, and it may not give you the best value for your advertising dollar. A more economical approach is desktop publishing. Ask around for the names of people who can design and print your brochure on their home computer. Here are some points to keep in mind if you want an advertising brochure.

- ✔ Because you generally have no longer than *20 seconds* to get someone's attention with printed advertisements, your message must be brief and to the point!
- ✔ Create a simple, straightforward layout.
- ✔ Repeat your phone number at least three times in large type.
- ✔ If your location is a selling feature, include a small map.
- ✔ Use paper that is heavy enough to be a self-mailer.
- ✔ Color is important.
- ✔ Photos are expensive.

## USE PAID ADVERTISING THOUGHTFULLY

Plan carefully when you use newspaper or telephone book advertising. Consider which days, and in which part of the newspaper, your customers are most likely to read your ad. Draft a simple classified ad here. Include the information that is most important to parents (price, location, ages served, special features), and try to catch their attention.

✎ _____

Examine the Yellow Pages to see who advertises there. Clip telephone book ads that you find especially effective. Like radio and television ads, telephone book advertising is very expensive, and it may not be effective for a child care business with a small customer base.

> "Business cards are cheap—I got 500 of them for less than $20! Now I include them with the Easter Egg Hunt candy I give out each year, making the candy a tax-deductible business expense."

# NETWORK FOR WORD-OF-MONTH ADVERTISING

A satisfied customer is the best advertisement! Parents are more comfortable with the recommendations of friends than with any advertising you do. Reward your customers when their referrals land you a new client. Also, get to know owners and employees of local businesses, especially small ones, whose workforce depends on child care. Word-of-mouth advertising will help promote your business faster than any other media.

Another approach for an individual child care business or an association of providers is to join the Chamber of Commerce. The Chamber welcomes small businesses as new members, and it may have mentor programs or other types of support available.

Finally, use your local child care resource and referral service. Get on its referral list, and ask the staff to activate your name when you anticipate a vacancy.

# FIND FREE ADVERTISING

It doesn't cost money to get your business in the public eye if you assume the role of child care professional and early-childhood expert in your community. You can use the newspaper's weekly professional announcement column to keep the name of your business in the news. The local media will often highlight child care shortages or innovative child care services in your community, so learn to draft a simple press release when you are expanding your business, holding a child care event at your facility, or participating in an important professional development activity.

## EXAMPLES

Mindy Meyer has expanded her child care business, Sweet Dreams Daycare, to serve infants as well as preschoolers. Ms. Meyer, who received her Associate's degree in child development this spring, participates in the Child and Adult Food Program and is currently Treasurer of the Downtown Child Care Association.

The Lowell School PTA Meeting will be held this Tuesday night, September 25, at 7 p.m. In the gymnasium. Guest speaker Laura Youngblood, owner of Kids' Club Child Care, will speak on the topic, "Finding Quality Child Care for Your School-Age Child."

Toon Town Commencement Ceremonies will be held on Saturday morning, June 12, at 9 a.m. Guest speaker Captain Kangaroo will address the graduating class of seven students as they prepare to enter kindergarten. Families and friends are invited to attend and to join alumni for the annual Toon Town Talent Show.

Ten Northside providers have joined the Babies First Child Care Network, expanding local child care options for infants and toddlers.

A shortage of infant care has challenged working parents. Community Care Center Director Margie Franklin reports, "Parents cannot work or complete welfare reform requirements when infant care is not available."

May 1 marks the Fourth Annual Worthy Wage Day Celebration, sponsored by the Middleburg Child Care Association. A lunch hour rally on the Courthouse lawn will be followed by a Family-Friendly Employer Fair at the Public Library.

"I'm excited by my new marketing calendar, and so are my customers. They will help spread the word about my high-quality child care service."

"You go, girl!"

## Homework Assignment

✔ Write a brief paragraph describing your business. Include services offered, years in business, anything that distinguishes your business from other child care businesses.

✔ Write a brief paragraph describing your background. How has it prepared you to operate your business successfully? Include your experience, education and training, credentials, and professional association memberships.

✔ Write a brief paragraph describing your geographic market. Discuss local demand for child care services in the area in which your business is located. How does this location serve your customers' needs?

✔ Write a brief paragraph describing your "typical" customer. Who primarily buys your service? Comment on the size and characteristics of your market. Why do customers purchase child care from you?

✔ Write a brief paragraph describing your child care services in your area. What separates your business from the competition?

✔ Describe how you market your business.

# 11

## COMMUNICATION LESSON

# Responsibilities of an Assertive Child Care Provider

Good relations between providers and parents are important not only to the profitability of child care businesses. They are equally important to the health and well-being of families. Children benefit when their provider is a well-trained professional, when care is stable and long lasting, and when parents demonstrate high levels of comfort and confidence in the provider.

Parents want to feel confident that their children's needs are being met with understanding and love and that their primary relationship with their child will never be usurped by another care giver. Parents and providers alike, however, are frequently unclear about their roles, their rights, and their responsibilities. Mutual understanding between parents and providers prepares both parties to participate in a more constructive partnership.

It is the professional responsibility of an assertive child care provider to support the primacy of parents in the lives of children. Only an unprofessional provider undermines parents by being openly critical of them or thinks she could replace parents in raising their children. Here are some potential concerns or anxieties that parents might have about placing their child in child care.

> **Note!**
>
> A provider who has a clear understanding of responsibilities, as well as rights, is well equipped to build strong partnerships with parents.

✔ Does my provider love and treat my child equally with other children, including her own?

✔ Is my child getting enough individualized attention?

✔ Am I missing out on the important moments and significant events of my child's life?

✔ Am I a bad mom for leaving my little baby with a "stranger" every day while I go to work?

✔ Does my provider talk about me and my family when I am not there?

## Brainstorming

### Responsibilities of a Child Care Provider/Business Owner

Put yourself in a parent's shoes, and list the responsibilities of a child care provider. Here are some examples to start you off.

✔ to develop a warm, loving relationship with every child

✔ to maintain a clean, safe, cheerful, and age-appropriate child care environment

✔ to never use harsh physical or emotional punishment when guiding the behavior of children

✔ to include parents in decisions about children

✔ to recognize and respect the different cultural, racial, and religious backgrounds of children's families

✔ to respect parents' privacy and confidentiality

✎ _____

✎ _____

✎ _____

✎ _____

✎ _____

"I spent a lot of time drafting this list, and now I give a copy of it to every parent with whom I work."

"The fact is that parents' days are long and tiring, their personal resources are limited, and it is easy for them to feel left out of the important child care moments in their child's life."

The communication skills we have reviewed will help you work more effectively with parents in the areas of business policies and practices. But this is just one small aspect of parent/provider relations. If you have not developed the parent/provider partnership as a critical component of your child care philosophy and practice, you are missing one of the most vital and effective strategies for improving the quality of your child care service. Check Appendix C for more resources on this topic.

# 12

# Your Child Care Business Plan

All of the homework assignments you have completed can now be compiled into a professional child care business plan. A business plan is a document that describes your business, your background, your policies and practices, your niche in the child care market, your customer profile, your marketing strategies, your profitability, and your financial strengths and weaknesses.

By assembling your homework into this simple nine-part business plan, you will be prepared to explain your business to anyone. If you want to apply for a loan or grant for your business, this preparation will help you make an excellent presentation. Do not hesitate to attach your business card, brochure, or other marketing and promotional materials to illustrate the healthy state of your business.

Your business plan is meant to be read by professionals, and it should be written in a detailed, business-like style. You may need to do some editing as you transcribe your homework assignments into your business plan. As you are writing, try to keep in mind the pin-striped bank loan officer or dollar-conscious grant manager who may someday review your business plan. This is not the place to share cute observations on your affinity for children and their antics!

If you are completing a business plan for the purpose of obtaining financing for your business, you should be able to answer the following questions:

> **Note!**
>
> You now have all the pieces of a professional business plan. Put them together, and you will be ready to describe your child care business practices and profitability to a banker, a small business loan center, or a grant funder.

- ✔ How much do you need to borrow, and how will this financing help your business be successful?
- ✔ How will you spend the borrowed money—on operating expenses, to purchase or repair equipment or furniture, to refinance your debt? Attach an itemized list if possible.

✔ What personal financial contribution have you made, or will you make, to this business?

✔ List the collateral you have available to secure the loan. What is the current value of the collateral?

Attach this additional information, along with a copy of your most recent federal income tax return, to your business plan.

# Child Care Business Plan

Name: _____

Address: _____

City: _____

State: _____

Zip Code: _____

Phone: _____

Business Name: _____

Date: _____

1. Describe your business. Include services offered, years in business, anything that distinguishes your business from other child care businesses. (Attach your business card.)

_____

_____

_____

_____

_____

2. Describe your background. How has it prepared you to operate your business successfully? Include your experience, education and training, credentials, and professional association memberships.

_____

_____

_____

_____

_____

# Child Care Business Plan (Continued)

3. Describe your geographic market. Discuss local demand for child care services in the area in which your business is located. How does this location serve your customers' needs?

_____

_____

_____

_____

4. Describe your "typical" customer. Who primarily buys your service? Comment on the size and characteristics of your market. Why do customers purchase child care services from you?

_____

_____

_____

_____

5. Describe other child care services in your area. What separates your business from the competition?

_____

_____

_____

_____

# Child Care Business Plan (Continued)

6. Describe how you market your business. (Attach marketing calendar and advertising materials.)

_____

_____

_____

_____

_____

7. Describe your current record-keeping system and business policies. How do these support the profitability of your business? (Attach a copy of your contract with parents.)

_____

_____

_____

_____

_____

8. Describe your business profitability. Is it profiting, breaking even, or losing money? Why is it in this position? (Attach your most recent annual income statement and balance sheet.)

_____

_____

_____

_____

_____

9. What will your income be for the next 12 months? Does your business have adequate cash flow to cover all expenses and meet your profit goals? (Attach your most recent cash flow plan and break-even analysis.)

_____

_____

_____

_____

_____

# Sample Business Documents

# Sample Renewal Child Care Contract

ANNUAL RENEWAL CONTRACT

Daisy Daycare

Susan Sanders, Child Care Provider
200 Daisy Avenue
Hamilton, MT

Beginning Date _____ through Ending Date _____

This renewal contract is made between the Parent/Guardian and Provider for the care of _____ at the home of Susan Sanders.

The fee is $_____ per hour/day. The times reserved are _____ for a total of _____ hours/days per week. The cost per week is $_____. Reserved times may be amended by mutual consent, with cost adjusted accordingly.

Payment is due on receipt of the monthly statement or any time between the first and eighth of the month following service. The total may include extra charges and/or reductions, as specified in Daisy Daycare's Annual Statement for Parents.

This contract may be terminated by either the Parent/Guardian or Provider by giving a two-week written notice in advance of the ending date. The Provider may immediately terminate the contract without giving any notice if the Parent/Guardian does not make payments when due.

The signature of the Parent/Guardian to this contract also indicates that he/she agrees to abide by the written policies of the Provider. The Provider may change these policies from time to time with notice.

Permission for in-house activity photos of child *is/is not* given by the Parent/Guardian.

This contract expires on the date of _____ .

_____          _____
Parent/Guardian Signature                                    Date

_____          _____
Home Address                                                         Telephone Number

_____          _____
Provider Signature                                                 Date

# Sample Seasonal Child Care Contract

## SUMMER CHILD CARE AGREEMENT

Summertime Child Care

Beginning Date _____ through Ending Date _____

Please reserve the weeks I have circled below for my child(ren) _____ for _____ days per week. I understand that by reserving these weeks I will be required to pay for the weeks circled, whether my child(ren) attend or not. I will not be charged for weeks not circled.

*Weeks:*    1    2    3    4    5    6    7    8    9    10    11    12

I also agree to pay the summer activity fee of $10.00 per month per family (increased fees during summer months cover costs of increased travel and activities), and I understand that the daily rate for summer care is $15.00 per child ($13.00 more for each additional child in my family). Payment will be made twice per month. Advance payment equal to the value of one payment period is required. Payment is due the fifth and twentieth of each month.

I *am/am not* interested in summer swim lessons to be held afternoons during Weeks 1 and 2 at the university. I will be responsible for the cost of the lessons if I wish my child to participate. Summertime Child Care will provide transportation at no additional cost.

Unless already paid, I agree to pay a one-time registration fee of $20.00 on or before the first day of my child's attendance.

I have read the above information as well as the Summertime Child Care brochure and agree to the payments described.

_____

Signature of Parent/Guardian            Date

_____

Signature of Provider            Date

# Sample Seasonal Child Care Contract (Continued)

SUMMER CHILD CARE AGREEMENT

## General information

The attached calendar shows the activities occurring each week. Many of the activities will be related to the theme of the week. Other activities will exercise the body rather than the mind. Your child(ren) will make their own decisions concerning the activities in which they wish to participate. Throughout the summer the children will be encouraged to put together a collection (rocks, leaves, insects, etc.). We also hope to reap the rewards of a successful garden. The week will be balanced between planned activities and free time to relax, play their own games, and enjoy the non-school days.

*Note:* We try to make all activities around rivers and ponds extremely safe and conservative. We stick to the shallow side waters of rivers where there is no current. Again, safety is our main concern, and we have extra teachers attend water field trips.

Binoculars, cameras, bug spray, and sunscreen lotions are all welcome. Please clearly and permanently label your child's name on anything you wish returned. We will always have child care bug spray and sunscreen lotion on hand if you do not wish to send these items.

Parents are always welcome to drop in for an activity or to chaperone a field trip. If you have any skills or ideas that may fit into a specific theme, let us know. We'd love to have your help!

# Sample Child Care Policy Statement

POLICIES

Victoria's TLC Daycare

Beginning Date _____ through Ending Date _____

Welcome to Victoria's TLC! I am honored that you have chosen me or are considering me as your child's care provider. I believe that being a child care provider is an extremely important profession. My most important goal is to nurture a strong sense of self-esteem in the children entrusted to my care. When we nurture self-respect in the children we encounter in our daily lives, we do a great service not only to these children as individuals, but to society as a whole.

My child care service is registered with the state to care for up to 12 children, plus 4 overlap children (after school or at lunch hour). I care for children from two-months old to school-age. I reserve just two of my spaces for infants under the age of two years. The children in my care enjoy being part of a mixed age group in a home-like environment. They participate in age-appropriate activities in my home, outdoors, and in the community. These activities encourage basic preschool skills.

I am a member of the State Child Care Association, the National Association for the Healthy Development of Young Children, and the La Leche League. I participate regularly in training programs sponsored by these groups and by the Child Care Resource & Referral Agency. I am certified in Infant/Child CPR and Emergency First Aid. I participate in the Child and Adult Care Food Program, and I offer nutritious meals and snacks to the children in my care. There is no smoking in my home. We have two friendly, tolerant, and declawed cats, "The Kid" and "Colette," and we plan to get a puppy in the next two years.

# SCHEDULE

| | |
|---|---|
| 7:30 to 9:15 | Breakfast and Free Play selections |
| 9:15 to 9:30 | Clean up |
| 9:30 to 10:30 | Circle Time (Organized activities such as stories, crafts, music—I play guitar, harmonica, and some banjo!—puppet shows, science demonstrations, concept development, etc.) |
| 10:30 to 12:00 | Outdoor Play (weather permitting) and Large Motor Activities (aerobics, games) |
| 12:00 to 12:45 | Lunch |
| 12:45 to 1:00 | Clean up |
| 1:00 to 3:00 | Naps and Quiet Time |
| 3:00 to 3:30 | Afternoon Snack |
| 3:30 to 4:00 | Circle Time |
| 4:00 to 5:00 | Indoors and Outdoors Free Play, occasional children's video or Sesame Street |
| 5:00 to 5:30 | Clean up and quiet activities |

This schedule gives you an idea of how your child's time will be spent in my home. This schedule is flexible depending on the children's ages, interests, and the weather. Infants have their own individual schedules. Sometimes we will go on field trips, which will change the daily schedule significantly. You will always know of these special trips in advance.

Hours: Victoria's TLC is open Monday through Friday from 7:30 a.m. to 5:30 p.m., 12 months of the year. Occasional evening and weekend care can be arranged in advance. My husband, John, works at the University, and I coordinate my vacation and holiday leave with his.

I am closed four holidays each year, each of which coincides with the State University holidays. These holidays are Thanksgiving Day and the following Friday; Memorial Day; and Independence Day.

In addition to these holidays, I take a total of four weeks' vacation leave each year. During these times, parents must arrange their own substitute care. My vacations will fall within these time periods:

✔ Christmas/New Year's recess

✔ Spring break

✔ Summer vacation

I will let my customers know of the exact dates of my vacations at least three months in advance.

*Sick and Emergency Closings:* If I am ill or my son Ryan is ill, I will call in an extra assistant from my regular staff of University student assistants to work for me. *Victoria's TLC will remain open and will be managed on these days by my assistants. I will, of course, be in my home and available to my assistants in case of emergency.* Some areas of my home are closed to the child care children, and these areas are where my family will stay in case of illness.

*Personal Days:* I reserve the right to take five paid personal days per year for family emergencies or to attend doctor's appointments, special family times, etc. During these personal days, Victoria's TLC will be closed. *If I must take an unexpected personal day, I will tell my customers as soon as possible,* and I will assist them in finding a back-up child care provider by sharing my back-up list. *If I need to take a personal day to attend a seminar or personal business, I will tell my customers four weeks in advance* so that they may plan their child's alternative care for that day.

## Rates, Payments, and Fees

**A message to my customers:** When I attended the Child Care Provider Orientation sponsored by Child Care Resource & Referral and the State Department of Family Services, I was told by the experts in the profession that the vast majority of complaints made by parents and providers regarding their child care experiences occur in the area of rates, payment, and fees. Many of our trainers at this seminar had been child care providers for 10 years or more, and their experience had taught them that clear financial policies and communication are a must. I also learned that one of the main reasons for the high turnover rate of child care providers is their dissatisfaction with their income, plus the confusion and conflicts with their customers in the area of money. Many excellent suggestions were offered on how to set up payment policies to prevent such problems. I have decided to take this advice and have set up my policies regarding rates, payment, and fees accordingly.

It is very important to me that my customers have a clear understanding of my policies. I realize that, even though I have tried to state them as clearly as possible, there will still be some questions. Please do not hesitate to ask me to clarify anything that is not clear to you—I will be happy to do so! Our parent/provider relationship is very important to me, and if there is anything I can do to enhance communication between us, I want to do it!

## Rates

Tuition is paid in 12 equal monthly installments due during the first week of every month. The monthly tuition is based on the following day and part-time rates.

*Full-time Day Rates:* A full-time day is from 7 to 10 hours

✔ *Infant Day Rate:* $20.00/day (for children under two years old)

✔ *Toddler/Preschool Day Rate:* $18.00/day

*Part-time Rates:* A part-time day is less than 7 hours

✔ *Infant Part-time Rate:* $2.50/hour

✔ *Toddler/Preschool Part-time Rate:* $2.00/hour

## Explanation of Monthly Tuition

Since January 1, 2XXX, Victoria's TLC has used a monthly payment plan. This plan helps parents better budget their child care costs. I calculate the total number of working days in a year (minus my unpaid vacation/holiday leave days) and multiply by your daily rate (full- or part-time, infant or preschooler). This I divide by 12, to arrive at your monthly rate.

## Cost-of-Living Adjustment

To keep up with inflation at least partially (which is 4 percent to 5 percent a year, according to the federal Social Security Administration), I reserve the right to adjust my rates annually in January. This increase will correspond to the annual cost-of-living index as calculated by the SSA. Customers will be informed of this rate increase at least three months in advance.

## Payment

The monthly tuition payment is due during the first week of every month of the year, or by the eighth of every month at the latest. A late fee will be charged for payments received after the eighth of the month. This tuition is my income and, to ensure that I can continue to care for your children, I ask that you plan on making your daycare payment on time.

I will distribute a monthly statement to each customer during the last week of every month; it will include all tuition and fees due by the eighth of the coming month.

The monthly tuition payment obligation is based on the hours you AGREE to use child care, not on the actual hours of attendance. Payment is due when you have agreed to use certain blocks of time, whether or not your child/ren actually attend during those hours. You are paying for a space reserved for your child/ren in Victoria's TLC Payment is due regardless of illnesses, your vacation, or holidays.

## Fees

*Enrollment Fee*: A one-time enrollment fee of $15.00 will be charged per child and is due with your first monthly tuition payment. This money will be used to replace broken toys, art supplies, books, etc.

*Late Payment Fee*: If a monthly tuition payment is not made by the eighth of the month, I will charge you a late fee of $25.00 and your child may not return to Victoria's TLC until all tuition and late fees are paid. After two late payments, I reserve the right to terminate our child care agreement.

*Overdrafts*: If a check is returned to me from the bank for any reason, I will charge a $25.00 overdraft fee, which must be paid after notification.

*Late Pick-Up*: Victoria's TLC closes at 5:30 p.m. All children must be picked up by that time. I will allow a five-minute grace period before charging for late pick-up. After 5:35 p.m., a fee of .50/minute will be charged. After three abuses of the closing hour, I may terminate our child care agreement. I ask that my customers please respect the closing hour, for the sake of my family.

*Note:* If you have a bona fide emergency and call to inform me that you will be late, I will make an exception for you. Also, I can occasionally care for a child after my closing hour by pre-arrangement. In these rare circumstances, I will charge my part-time rate for your child care after 5:30 p.m.

## Admission

A parent interview is required before acceptance to Victoria's TLC I will need to keep on file your child/ren's Medical Record, Emergency Contact and Parental Consent Form, Parent/Provider Contract, Authorization to Leave Care Form, Field Trip Permission Slip, and Child and Adult Care Food Program Enrollment Form. All immunizations must be current, and infants under the age of two years must have a pre-admission physical within two weeks of admission.

## Meals

I will provide breakfast, lunch, and an afternoon snack. All meals and snacks will be in compliance with the nutritional standards set by the Child and Adult Care Food Program. If a special diet is required, the necessary foods must be provided by the parent.

✔ Birthdays are special days, so you may bring cake, cookies, or other treats to help celebrate!

✔ Parents of infants may provide expressed breast milk. I will provide formula or baby food. Bottles, baby cups, spoons, and pacifiers must be supplied by parents. *Please label bottles.*

# Sample Child Care Policy Statement (Continued)

## Health Issues

I will follow the Pediatricians' Recommendations for Exclusion from Daycare Guidelines, which will be given to you at enrollment. If you aren't sure whether to bring your child to child care, please call me in the morning and we will make a decision. Sick children will be refused care. This policy helps to protect your child from exposure to communicable disease.

Scratches and scrapes are inevitable when children play, and they will be treated with antiseptic, a band-aid, and extra TLC. For anything more serious, I will contact you immediately and expect you to pick up your child ASAP. Sick children will be isolated until their parent or authorized escort arrives. If your job makes you unavailable by phone, please leave an Emergency Consent on file at Community Medical Center and notify me of it.

I am certified in Infant/Child CPR and Emergency First Aid. If a situation calls for such serious measures, I will call 911 and inform you ASAP that your child has been transported to the hospital. I carry Accident Insurance, which will cover the first $5,000 of Emergency Care for your child including ambulance transport, if your own insurance does not cover these items.

Medications must have a parental consent form listing the dosage and medication schedule. All medications must be in their original container with the original label. This is for your child's protection.

## Clothing, Diapers, and Supplies

Each child will have his/her own storage shelf in my home. Parents will be responsible for providing the following:

✔ *Diapers and Wipes.* Either disposable or cloth diapers are acceptable. If you choose to use cloth diapers, I require you to provide an *AIRTIGHT* container for dirty diapers (for example, a heavy-duty zip-lock storage bag). You must bring this container with you in the morning and take it home with you each evening. Also, if you choose to use cloth diapers, please provide pinless diaper wraps rather than pins and plastic pants. Please keep your child's shelf adequately supplied with diapers. There will be a charge of .75 per TLC diaper used on your child if his/her supply runs out.

✔ *Complete Set of Extra Clothing.* Please leave a complete set of clothing appropriate for the season at my home on your child's shelf. If your child requires a change of clothing during the day, I will send the soiled clothing home with you and ask that you replace the extra set the next day. Please also leave a plastic bag on your child's shelf for soiled clothes.

✔ *Complete Set of Extra Clothing.* Please leave a complete set of clothing appropriate for the season at my home on your child's shelf. If your child requires a change of clothing during the day, I will send the soiled clothing home with you and ask that you replace the extra set the next day. Please also leave a plastic bag on your child's shelf for soiled clothes.

✔ *Additional Notes about Clothing.* Please dress your child so that he or she does not have to worry about getting dirty. No bare feet, please. Also, please send your child with *empty pockets.* Victoria's TLC will not be responsible for small articles that are lost.

✔ *Blanket* for infants; *Blanket, Pillow, and Mat/pad* for toddlers. Infants will nap in cribs/playpens, which I will provide. A favorite toy, stuffed animal, or pacifier is fine. *Please label everything.*

## Child Guidance Policy

I believe positive reinforcement is a much more effective way of encouraging desirable behavior than negative reinforcement. No corporal punishment will be used. Time-out/quiet chair may be used along with discussion of the incident in terms the child can understand. If there is a problem, I will discuss it with you, and we will work together to resolve the situation.

## Authorized Escorts

For your child's safety, I can allow your child to leave my home only with (1) you (the person(s) enrolling the child), (2) persons you specify on the authorization to Leave Care Form, and (3) *in an emergency*, a person who is not on the list if you have told me in person or by phone that he or she is picking up your child and if I have a signed and dated note from you authorizing me to send your child home with that person.

Also, your child must be brought to my door and I must be told that he or she has arrived. He or she must be picked up at the door and I must be told the child is leaving.

## Transportation

Please fill out a Field Trip Permission Form so that your child can enjoy occasional field trips with us. When transporting your children by car, they will be placed in proper child safety restraints or seat belts (depending on the child's size). I may ask you to provide a small fee for bus fare, museum admission, etc.

## Annual Update

I will ask you to fill out new forms annually. It is extremely important that these forms be returned to me by the deadlines I specify. Please let me know immediately if your name, address, or phone number changes so that my records are always accurate.

## Additional Parent Responsibilities

*I ask that parents assume these responsibilities:*

- ✔ To provide 15 days' notice in writing before withdrawing a child for any reason (except for serious medical emergency). If a parent withdraws a child suddenly without giving notice, the parent will pay one-half month's tuition after child's withdrawal.

- ✔ To provide 30 days' notice in writing before attempting to change the permanent child care schedule stated in the Parent/Provider Contract. If 30 days' notice is not given and requested changes involve decreased child care hours, the parent will pay tuition for the previously agreed-upon schedule for the month. If the requested changes involve increased hours, I will try to accommodate it, although this may not be possible. The more advance notice you give me, the better the chance of my being able to accommodate your changes.

- ✔ To consistently communicate with me about any changes in the child's behavior or life that can affect him or her, so that I may best meet his or her emotional and physical needs. For example, if a favorite pet dies, I would like to know. That way I can be sensitive to your child's needs and feelings.

- ✔ It is necessary that we keep my neighbors' driveways clear and that you park in legal parking areas in front of my home. Please do not double park. Help me to maintain good relationships with my neighbors.

## Additional Provider Responsibilities

*I will assume these responsibilities:*

- ✔ To provide a nurturing, responsible, licensed, and safe child care home that supports the emotional, social, intellectual, and physical needs of your child.

- ✔ To provide at least two weeks' notice in writing before ending care for any child, unless it is because of delinquent payment by the parent, in which case care will cease immediately until all child care bills have been paid in full.

✔ To provide written daily records for all infants (children under two years of age) so that you will know when your infant has eaten and how much, if he or she has had a bowel movement, etc. For both infants and toddlers/preschoolers, I will always let parents know of any behavior that occurs in my care that is out of the ordinary for your child (for example, if he or she slept or cried more than usual).

✔ To provide monthly and yearly receipts of payments for parent's tax purposes.

## A Final Note to My Customers

I have written all of these policies to enhance clear communication in our parent/provider relationship and so that both of us know what is expected of us in our cooperative effort to provide Victoria's TLC children with the very best child care experience possible. If you have any questions about any of these policies, please feel free to ask me now or at any time in the future. Our relationship is very important to me. Please communicate your ideas and needs with me on a regular basis. I thank you from the bottom of my heart for entrusting me to provide care for your precious child/ren. I vow to do my very best to provide him or her with a wonderful and loving experience in my home

TINY TOTS FAMILY CHILD CARE
PROFESSIONAL BUSINESS PLAN

*Name:* Jamie M. Dower

*Address:* 101 Easy Street East Missoula, MT 59806 (406)549-0001

*Business Name:* Tiny Tots Family Child Care Date: October 1, 2XXX

## Description of Business

Tiny Tots is a Family Child Care Home that is licensed to provide care to six children, ages birth to five years. State Department of Family Services regulations allow one adult to care for six children. Primary caregiver and business manager is Jamie Dower. Tiny Tots serves three children under two years of age, and three children over two years. The business is located in the Dower home at 101 Easy Street, East Missoula, Montana. The house is bright and airy with 2000 square feet, 2 × 12 construction, aluminum siding, Therma-pane windows, two bathrooms, and a large backyard 107′ by 70′, fully enclosed by chain-link fencing. Tiny Tots has been in business since March 1995.

## Background

Several years ago, after successfully raising five children, I investigated the possibility of buying a building to start a child care center. Because of the amount of capital required I did not pursue that possibility at that time. Instead, I started a child care business in my own home, which is large, includes a yard that meets child care requirements, and is conveniently located. I became registered with the State Department of Family Services to care for six children. After completing the full-day Child Care Provider Orientation Training offered by Child Care Resources in Missoula, I participated in more than 30 hours of early childhood training during each of the past two years. This year I am enrolled as a University of Montana student in the Associate's degree program in the child development. I am a member of the Montana Child Care Association (MCCA), and I serve as a Board Member to that organization's Missoula Chapter. I am also a member of the National Association of Education for Young Children (NAEYC). I am certified in Pediatric CPR and First Aid.

Previous to my child care work, I worked for eight years as the general manager of our family-owned business, the Lucky J Motel. I supervised the housekeepers, ordered supplies, managed the front desk, and kept the books.

### Local Market

Missoula's child care industry continues to grow as more and more mothers enter the workforce. In the Missoula area, the number of child care providers has increased every year for the past seven years. East Missoula has increased its population by 25 percent over the past four years. According to Child Care Resources Resource & Referral Service, which matches families needing child care with caregivers, there is a shortage of registered child care in East Missoula.

The location of a child care business is important to parents. They look for child care close to their homes and jobs and close to their children's school. My location is convenient for parents in the Mount Jumbo area; it is close to Mount Jumbo School and to the convenience/grocery store where families stop after school and work.

### Customer Profile

My market consists primarily of working parents of young children who live in and around East Missoula. These parents work full or part time. Their places of employment are located in the City of Missoula, requiring a 15- to 30-minute commute each way. My child care service is conveniently located near their homes. I offer these families high-quality, experienced infant care and toddler/preschooler care, as well as part-day care for kindergartners at Mount Jumbo school. Transportation to and from Mount Jumbo School is provided. Meals and snacks are included free of charge, and they meet the nutritional guidelines of the USDA Child and Adult Care Food Program. My service is especially convenient to families with multiple children, whose multi-aged siblings can attend the same child care facility.

### Other Child Care Services in Local Market

There are only four other child care businesses in East Missoula, according to staff at Child Care Resources. Two of these are Group Home Day Cares, licensed to care for 12 children and not able to offer the more intimate, home-like environment of Tiny Tots. Two other competitors are located on the outskirts of East Missoula, and neither of these offers the security of a fully fenced outdoor play area. Further, I am the only East Missoula child care provider to seriously pursue continued education in the field of early childhood development.

## Business Policies

I keep a monthly ledger to record income and expenses, all of which flow through a Tiny Tots business checking account. My contract with parents is renewed annually. It clearly states Tiny Tot's monthly rates and payment schedule, activity fees, and penalty fees for late child pick-up and late payment. Parents agree to pay for all hours of care reserved, with a 10-day annual limit on unpaid child absences for vacation or illness. At the time of enrollment parents pay a one-month security deposit, which will be fully refunded if 30 days' notice of termination is given, as specified in my contract. Monthly payment is made in advance. These policies ensure that my income remains stable throughout the year. My rates and fees are based on a market survey of East Missoula child care facilities, and they fall at the upper end of the range while remaining competitive for infant care. Parents agree to secure substitute care during my two-week vacation in July and for five days at Christmas.

## Marketing

My best marketing tool has been word-of-mouth from satisfied customers, which is extremely effective in the small community of East Missoula. When I anticipate vacancies at Tiny Tots, I activate my referral listing with Child Care Resources, so that families needing care in the East Missoula area are given my name and address. At these times, I also run classified ads in the Child Care Services section of the Sunday *Missoulian* and the weekly *Messenger*, and I post flyers in and around Mount Jumbo School.

## Profitability

Since the beginning of its second year in business, Tiny Tots has earned a small but steady monthly profit. I have been able to pay myself a monthly wage of $1,100, plus meet my profit goal of $2,000/year. In September of 1995 I implemented an increase in my rates for part-time and infant care, and in January 1997 I added to my contract an annual cost-of-living adjustment based on the federal Social Security Administration cost-of-living Index. I further maximize my income by participating in the Child and Adult Care Food Program, which reimburses me an average of $365/month.

## Income Projections

Based on Tiny Tots' financial records for the past two years, I anticipate monthly income to range from $2,000 to $2,400. Monthly expenses, including wages and taxes, will be approximately $1,800.

# Sample Child Care Business Plan 2

PLAY PLACE CHILD CARE BUSINESS PLAN

*Name:* Xue Vang

*Address:* 120 Turner Street Garden City, MT 59802 (406) 728-5555

*Business Name:* Play Place Child Care        Date: September 2, 2XXX

## Description of Business

Play Place is a family home child care service, registered since 1994 with the State Department of Family Services to care for six children. Caregiver and manager is Xue Vang. Play Place is located in the refinished garage of the Vang family residence at 120 Turner Street on the Northside of Garden City. The facility has 1,000 square feet available for child care. The construction is $2 \times 12$, with a bathroom and large fenced yard. After three successful years, Play Place is registering as a Group Home Day Care, which can serve up to 12 children with the assistance of 2 part-time staff.

## Background

After moving to the United States in 1982, I learned English and in 1992 earned a Graduate Equivalency Degree through the Garden City School District Adult Basic Education Program. While I was caring for my own two children at home, I recognized the need for high-quality child care in my Northside neighborhood. Since the opening of Play Place, I have attended Child Care Orientation, annual Child and Adult Care Food Program trainings, and monthly Garden City Child Care Association trainings. This year I participated in the six-week Child Care Business Training at Garden City Economic Development Group.

## Local Market

The Northside is home to many families with young children. I live across the street from a school-bus stop for students of Lincoln Elementary School, kindergarten through fifth grade. Every morning more than 25 children board the bus here. Only six blocks away is Whitman School, site of Garden City's Head Start part-day preschool programs. In my residential neighborhood there are many houses and apartments belonging to the Garden City Housing Authority, which provides subsidized housing to low-income families. Also nearby are Mountain Sports factory and St. John's Hospital, which employ many of my neighbors. Play Place's location and hours of service make it convenient to shift workers, such as Mountain Sports factory and St. John's employees, and to families whose children attend Lincoln School or Head Start.

## Customer Profile

My customers are primarily Northside families with children from birth to 12 years old. They work or participate in job training activities through the Garden City Job Service. Many of them need part-time care, and many of them need shift care beginning at 7 a.m. or ending at 11:30 p.m. Play Place specializes in scheduling part-time care and offers early-morning and late-night care.

## Other Child Care Services in Local Market

There are two relatively new Family Home Day Cares on the Northside. The Northside's only child care center closed last January, leaving many families here in need of child care. I am the most experienced child care provider in this area. According to the Child Care Resource & Referral Agency, I am the only provider who uses a contract and policy statement. I pride myself on the stability of my business, my good relations with families, and my well-kept child care facility and outdoor play area. I am also the only facility offering early-morning and late-night child care.

## Business Policies

I use a monthly ledger to track all income and expenses. Because I offer part-time, early-morning, and late-night care, I am able to price my rates slightly higher than those of my competitors. I am happy to work with customers whose payment is assisted by the state, but I require that they make up the difference between the state rate and my rate. I bill for services every month, use a monthly rate, and ask for one-month payment in advance. Customers agree to limit unpaid child absence days to 10/year. I am reimbursed approximately $650/month by the Child and Adult Care Food Program.

## Marketing

Play Place is listed with the local Child Care Resource & Referral Service. I have displayed my flyers at the office at Lincoln School, Garden City JOBS Service, and Garden City Housing Authority Resident Council Office. Staff at these offices regularly refer clients to me for child care.

## Profitability

Play Place has broken even or made a profit every year for the past three years. This year, with the expansion to Group Home and the addition of my two nieces to my staff, I project income that will allow me to pay myself $1,100/month, pay my helpers each $910/month, and reach my monthly profit goal of $100.

### Income Projections

Income for the next 12 months is projected at $46,800 from tuition and $7,800 from the Child and Adult Care Food Program, totaling $54,600. Operational expenses are projected at $1,200/month (or $14,400/year); variable expenses will be $3,150/month or ($37,800/year). This projects an annual profit of $2,400. Because this calculation was based on a full-time equivalency of only 10 children, it is a conservative projection. I believe this profit would be adequate to allow me to repay debt on an $10,000 business loan for structural improvements to my child care facility.

# B

# Reproducible Forms

# Market Rate Survey Chart

### Daily Rates

| Number of Providers | $ | $ | $ | $ | $ | $ |
|---|---|---|---|---|---|---|
| | | | | | | |
| | | | | | | |
| | | | | | | |
| | | | | | | |
| | | | | | | |

# Child Care Contract

Program Name _____

Name of Parent(s) or Guardian(s) _____

Name of Child Enrolled _____ Birth Date _____

Address _____ City _____

State _____ ZIP Code _____ Phone Number _____

Name, Address, Phone of Adults with Whom You Agree to Work

_____

_____

_____

Days and Hours of Reserved Care _____

_____

Rates and Payment Schedule _____

_____

Scheduled and Unscheduled Child Absences _____

_____

Third-Party Payers _____

_____

Termination Policy _____

_____

Penalty Fees _____

_____

# Child Care Contract (Continued)

Supplemental Fees _____

Provider Leave (Holiday, Vacation, Sick) _____

Substitute Care Arrangements _____

Date of Contract Renegotiation _____

*Attached:* Emergency Medical Information/Release Form

❏ name and telephone number of child's physician

❏ name and telephone number of child's dentist

❏ health insurance policy number

❏ special disabilities, medical conditions, or dietary information

❏ alternative emergency contact name and telephone number

*Attached:* Sick Child Exclusion Policy

# Break-Even Analysis

**Monthly Direct Costs** (Expenses that depend on the number of children you serve)
Food . . . . . . . . . . . . . . . . . . . . . . . . . . . . . . . . . . . . . . . . . . . . $ _____
Materials . . . . . . . . . . . . . . . . . . . . . . . . . . . . . . . . . . . . . . . . $ _____
Labor . . . . . . . . . . . . . . . . . . . . . . . . . . . . . . . . . . . . . . . . . . . $ _____

Plus

**Monthly Operating Costs** (These expenses don't vary month to month)
Advertising . . . . . . . . . . . . . . . . . . . . . . . . . . . . . . . . . . . . . . . $ _____
Arts and Crafts Supplies . . . . . . . . . . . . . . . . . . . . . . . . . . . . $ _____
Dues/Subscriptions . . . . . . . . . . . . . . . . . . . . . . . . . . . . . . . . $ _____
Insurance . . . . . . . . . . . . . . . . . . . . . . . . . . . . . . . . . . . . . . . . $ _____
Maintenance/Repairs . . . . . . . . . . . . . . . . . . . . . . . . . . . . . . $ _____
Office Supplies . . . . . . . . . . . . . . . . . . . . . . . . . . . . . . . . . . . . $ _____
Rent . . . . . . . . . . . . . . . . . . . . . . . . . . . . . . . . . . . . . . . . . . . . $ _____
Telephone . . . . . . . . . . . . . . . . . . . . . . . . . . . . . . . . . . . . . . . $ _____
Wages (For staff who don't work directly with children) . . . . . . . . . . $ _____
Training . . . . . . . . . . . . . . . . . . . . . . . . . . . . . . . . . . . . . . . . . $ _____
Other . . . . . . . . . . . . . . . . . . . . . . . . . . . . . . . . . . . . . . . . . . . $ _____

Plus

**Other Cash Needs** (Debt payment, taxes) . . . . . . . . . . . . . . . . . . . $ _____

Plus

**Profit Goal** (Your decision) . . . . . . . . . . . . . . . . . . . . . . . . . . . . . $ _____

Equals

**Break-Even Point** . . . . . . . . . . . . . . . . . . . . . . . . . . . . . . . . . . . . $ _____

Now calculate:

**Break-Even Point** . . . . . . . . . . . . . . . . . . . . . . . . . . . . . . . . . . . . $ _____
**Divided by Number of Children Served Per Month**
(Limited by state regulations) . . . . . . . . . . . . . . . . . . . . . . . . . . . . $ _____

Equals

**Average Monthly Income Needed Per Child** . . . . . . . . . . . . . . . . . $ _____

# Child Care Ledger Worksheet

## Ledger Spreadsheet

| | Income | | | | | | | DATE | Checks Issued To & Deposit Descriptions | In Payment Of | Check # | Amount of Check | Expenses | | |
|---|---|---|---|---|---|---|---|---|---|---|---|---|---|---|---|
| Miscellaneous | | Child Care Tuition | USDA Food Program | Amount of Deposit | Balance | | | | | | | | Food | Supplies —Mat'ls | Maint Repair |
| Descr. | Amt. | | | | | | | | ←BROUGHT FORWARD→ | | | | | | |
| | | | | | | | | | | | | | | | |
| | | | | | | | | | | | | | | | |
| | | | | | | | | | | | | | | | |
| | | | | | | | | | | | | | | | |
| | | | | | | | | | | | | | | | |
| | | | | | | | | | | | | | | | |
| | | | | | | | | | | | | | | | |
| | | | | | | | | | | | | | | | |
| | | | | | | | | | | | | | | | |
| | | | | | | | | | | | | | | | |
| | | | | | | | | | | | | | | | |
| | | | | | | | | | | | | | | | |
| | | | | | | | | | | | | | | | |
| | | | | | | | | | | | | | | | |
| | | | | | | | | | | | | | | | |
| | | | | | | | | | | | | | | | |
| | | | | | | | | | | | | | | | |
| | | | | | | | | | | | | | | | |

# Child Care Cash Flow Projection

**Business Name:**
**For Year Of:**

| Month: | Jan | Feb | Mar | Apr | May | June | July | Aug | Sep | Oct | Nov | Dec | Total |
|---|---|---|---|---|---|---|---|---|---|---|---|---|---|
| **Slots filled:** | | | | | | | | | | | | | |
| Revenue | | | | | | | | | | | | | |
| Tuition | | | | | | | | | | | | | |
| USDA | | | | | | | | | | | | | |
| Other | | | | | | | | | | | | | |
| TOTAL | | | | | | | | | | | | | |
| Direct Costs | | | | | | | | | | | | | |
| Labor/ Employment Taxes | | | | | | | | | | | | | |
| Substitute | | | | | | | | | | | | | |
| Food | | | | | | | | | | | | | |
| Other | | | | | | | | | | | | | |
| TOTAL | | | | | | | | | | | | | |
| Direct Cost % | | | | | | | | | | | | | |
| GROSS PROFIT | | | | | | | | | | | | | |
| Gross Profit % | | | | | | | | | | | | | |
| Operating Costs | | | | | | | | | | | | | |
| Advertising | | | | | | | | | | | | | |
| Bank Fees | | | | | | | | | | | | | |
| Child Care Supplies | | | | | | | | | | | | | |
| Dues/ Subscriptions | | | | | | | | | | | | | |
| Insurance | | | | | | | | | | | | | |
| Maintenance/ Repair | | | | | | | | | | | | | |
| Mileage | | | | | | | | | | | | | |
| Miscellaneous | | | | | | | | | | | | | |
| Office Supplies | | | | | | | | | | | | | |
| Payroll Taxes | | | | | | | | | | | | | |
| Postage | | | | | | | | | | | | | |
| Printing | | | | | | | | | | | | | |

# Child Care Cash Flow Projection (Continued)

**Business Name:**
**For Year Of:**

| Month: | Jan | Feb | Mar | Apr | May | June | July | Aug | Sep | Oct | Nov | Dec | Total |
|---|---|---|---|---|---|---|---|---|---|---|---|---|---|
| Professional Services | | | | | | | | | | | | | |
| Rent | | | | | | | | | | | | | |
| Taxes/Licenses | | | | | | | | | | | | | |
| Telephone | | | | | | | | | | | | | |
| Travel | | | | | | | | | | | | | |
| Training | | | | | | | | | | | | | |
| Utilities | | | | | | | | | | | | | |
| Wages/ Administration | | | | | | | | | | | | | |
| TOTAL | | | | | | | | | | | | | |
| NET PROFIT | | | | | | | | | | | | | |
| Net Profit % | | | | | | | | | | | | | |
| Beginning Cash | | | | | | | | | | | | | |
| PLUS: | | | | | | | | | | | | | |
| Net Profit | | | | | | | | | | | | | |
| Loan Proceeds | | | | | | | | | | | | | |
| Equity Injection | | | | | | | | | | | | | |
| Grants Received | | | | | | | | | | | | | |
| Donations | | | | | | | | | | | | | |
| Other | | | | | | | | | | | | | |
| SUBTOTAL | | | | | | | | | | | | | |
| LESS: | | | | | | | | | | | | | |
| Debt Service (P & I) | | | | | | | | | | | | | |
| Capital Expenditure | | | | | | | | | | | | | |
| Major Equipment | | | | | | | | | | | | | |
| Income Tax | | | | | | | | | | | | | |
| Owner Draw | | | | | | | | | | | | | |
| SUBTOTAL | | | | | | | | | | | | | |
| Surplus <Deficit> | | | | | | | | | | | | | |
| Ending Cash | | | | | | | | | | | | | |

# Income Statement

**Name of Program:**

**For period from** _____ , 20__ to ___, 20__

Child Care Revenue. . . . . . . . . . . . . . . . . . . . . . . . . . . . . . . . . . . $ _____

Minus Direct Costs . . . . . . . . . . . . . . . . . . . . . . . . . . . . . . . . . − _____

Equals Gross Profit . . . . . . . . . . . . . . . . . . . . . . . . . . . . . . . . = _____


Gross Profit . . . . . . . . . . . . . . . . . . . . . . . . . . . . . . . . . . . . . . $ _____

Minus Operating Costs . . . . . . . . . . . . . . . . . . . . . . . . . . . . . − _____

Equals Net Profit. . . . . . . . . . . . . . . . . . . . . . . . . . . . . . . . . . = _____


Net Profit . . . . . . . . . . . . . . . . . . . . . . . . . . . . . . . . . . . . . . . . $ _____

Minus Capital Expenditures. . . . . . . . . . . . . . . . . . . . . . . . . − _____

Minus Interest Expense. . . . . . . . . . . . . . . . . . . . . . . . . . . . . − _____

Minus Depreciation . . . . . . . . . . . . . . . . . . . . . . . . . . . . . . . − _____

Equals Income Before Taxes . . . . . . . . . . . . . . . . . . . . . . . . = _____


Income Before Taxes. . . . . . . . . . . . . . . . . . . . . . . . . . . . . . . $ _____

Minus Income Tax Expenses. . . . . . . . . . . . . . . . . . . . . . . . − _____

Equals Net Income . . . . . . . . . . . . . . . . . . . . . . . . . . . . . . . . = _____

# Balance Sheet

Statement of Assets and Liabilities as of _____, 20___

**Program Name:**

| ASSETS | | LIABILITIES | |
|---|---|---|---|
| **Current Assets** | | **Current Liabilities** | |
| Cash . . . . . . . . . . . . . . . . . $ _____ | | Accounts Payable . . . . . . . $ _____ | |
| Accounts Receivable . . . . . . + _____ | | Income Tax Payable . . . . . . + _____ | |
| Inventory . . . . . . . . . . . . . + _____ | | Short-Term Loan Payable . . + _____ | |
| Prepaid Expenses . . . . . . . . + _____ | | Current Portion, Long-Term + _____ | |
| Total Current Assets . . . . . . $ _____ | | Total Current Liabilities . . . . $ _____ | |
| **Fixed Assets** | | **Long-Term Liabilities** | |
| Land, Building, Equipment, and Furniture . . . . . . . . . . . $ _____ | | Long-Term Loan Payable . . $ _____ | |
| Less Depreciation . . . . . . . . − _____ | | Other . . . . . . . . . . . . . . . . . + _____ | |
| Total Fixed Assets . . . . . . . . $ _____ | | Total Long-Term Liabilities $ _____ | |
| **Total Current Assets** . . . . . $ _____ | | **Total Current Liabilities** $ _____ | |
| **Total Fixed Assets** . . . . . . + _____ | | **Total Long-Term Liabilities** + _____ | |
| **TOTAL ASSETS** . . . . . . . . $ _____ | | **TOTAL LIABILITIES** . . . . $ _____ | |
| | | **OWNER'S EQUITY** . . . . . $ _____ | |
| TOTAL ASSETS . . . . . . . . . . $ _____ | = | TOTAL LIABILITIES + OWNER'S EQUITY . . . . . . . $ _____ | |

# Child Care Business Plan

Name: _____

Address: _____

City: _____

State: _____

Zip Code: _____

Phone: _____

Business Name: _____

Date: _____

1. *Describe your business. Include type of service offered, years in business, anything that separates your business from other child care businesses. (Attach your business card.)*

   _____

   _____

   _____

   _____

2. *Describe your background. How has it prepared you to operate your business successfully? Include your experience, education and training, credentials and professional association memberships.*

   _____

   _____

   _____

3. *Describe your geographic market. Discuss local demand for child care services in the area in which your business is located. How does this location serve your customer's needs?*

   _____

   _____

   _____

   _____

# Child Care Business Plan (Continued)

4. *Describe your "typical customer. Who primarily buys your service? Comment on the size and characteristics of your market. Why do customers purchase child care services from you?*

5. *Describe other child care services in your area. What separates your business from the competition.*

6. *Describe how you market your business. (Attach marketing calendar and advertising materials.*

7. *Describe your current record-keeping system and business policies. How do these support the profitability of your business? (Attach your contract.)*

# Child Care Business Plan (Continued)

8. *Describe your business profitability. Is it profiting, breaking even, or losing money? Why is it in this position? (Attach your most recent annual income statement and balance sheet.)*

_____

_____

_____

_____

9. *What will your income be fore the next 12 months? Does your business have adequate cash flow to cover all expenses and meet your profit goals? (Attach your most recent cash flow plan and break-even analysis.)*

_____

_____

_____

_____

# Child Care Ledger Worksheet

## Ledger Spreadsheet

| | Income | | | | DATE | Checks Issued To & Deposit Descriptions | In Payment Of | Check # | Amount of Check | Expenses | | |
|---|---|---|---|---|---|---|---|---|---|---|---|---|
| Miscellaneous | | Child Care Tuition | USDA Food Program | Amount of Deposit | Balance | | | | | Food | Supplies —Mat'ls | Maint Repair |
| Descr. | Amt. | | | | | | | | | | | |
| | | | | | | ←BROUGHT FORWARD→ | | | | | | |
| | | | | | | | | | | | | |
| | | | | | | | | | | | | |
| | | | | | | | | | | | | |
| | | | | | | | | | | | | |
| | | | | | | | | | | | | |
| | | | | | | | | | | | | |
| | | | | | | | | | | | | |
| | | | | | | | | | | | | |
| | | | | | | | | | | | | |
| | | | | | | | | | | | | |
| | | | | | | | | | | | | |
| | | | | | | | | | | | | |

# Child Care Cash Flow Projection

**Business Name:**
**For Year Of:**

| Month: | Jan | Feb | Mar | Apr | May | June | July | Aug | Sep | Oct | Nov | Dec | Total |
|---|---|---|---|---|---|---|---|---|---|---|---|---|---|
| **Slots filled:** | | | | | | | | | | | | | |
| Revenue | | | | | | | | | | | | | |
| Tuition | | | | | | | | | | | | | |
| USDA | | | | | | | | | | | | | |
| Other | | | | | | | | | | | | | |
| TOTAL | | | | | | | | | | | | | |
| Direct Costs | | | | | | | | | | | | | |
| Labor/ Employment Taxes | | | | | | | | | | | | | |
| Substitute | | | | | | | | | | | | | |
| Food | | | | | | | | | | | | | |
| Other | | | | | | | | | | | | | |
| TOTAL | | | | | | | | | | | | | |
| Direct Cost % | | | | | | | | | | | | | |
| GROSS PROFIT | | | | | | | | | | | | | |
| Gross Profit % | | | | | | | | | | | | | |
| Operating Costs | | | | | | | | | | | | | |
| Advertising | | | | | | | | | | | | | |
| Bank Fees | | | | | | | | | | | | | |
| Child Care Supplies | | | | | | | | | | | | | |
| Dues/ Subscriptions | | | | | | | | | | | | | |
| Insurance | | | | | | | | | | | | | |
| Maintenance/ Repair | | | | | | | | | | | | | |
| Mileage | | | | | | | | | | | | | |
| Miscellaneous | | | | | | | | | | | | | |
| Office Supplies | | | | | | | | | | | | | |
| Payroll Taxes | | | | | | | | | | | | | |
| Postage | | | | | | | | | | | | | |
| Printing | | | | | | | | | | | | | |

# Child Care Cash Flow Projection (Continued)

**Business Name:**
**For Year Of:**

| Month: | Jan | Feb | Mar | Apr | May | June | July | Aug | Sep | Oct | Nov | Dec | Total |
|---|---|---|---|---|---|---|---|---|---|---|---|---|---|
| Professional Services | | | | | | | | | | | | | |
| Rent | | | | | | | | | | | | | |
| Taxes/Licenses | | | | | | | | | | | | | |
| Telephone | | | | | | | | | | | | | |
| Travel | | | | | | | | | | | | | |
| Training | | | | | | | | | | | | | |
| Utilities | | | | | | | | | | | | | |
| Wages/ Administration | | | | | | | | | | | | | |
| TOTAL | | | | | | | | | | | | | |
| NET PROFIT | | | | | | | | | | | | | |
| Net Profit % | | | | | | | | | | | | | |
| Beginning Cash | | | | | | | | | | | | | |
| PLUS: | | | | | | | | | | | | | |
| Net Profit | | | | | | | | | | | | | |
| Loan Proceeds | | | | | | | | | | | | | |
| Equity Injection | | | | | | | | | | | | | |
| Grants Received | | | | | | | | | | | | | |
| Donations | | | | | | | | | | | | | |
| Other | | | | | | | | | | | | | |
| SUBTOTAL | | | | | | | | | | | | | |
| LESS: | | | | | | | | | | | | | |
| Debt Service (P & I) | | | | | | | | | | | | | |
| Capital Expenditure | | | | | | | | | | | | | |
| Major Equipment | | | | | | | | | | | | | |
| Income Tax | | | | | | | | | | | | | |
| Owner Draw | | | | | | | | | | | | | |
| SUBTOTAL | | | | | | | | | | | | | |
| Surplus <Deficit> | | | | | | | | | | | | | |
| Ending Cash | | | | | | | | | | | | | |

# Income Statement

**Name of Program:**

**For period from** _____, 20__ to ___, 20__

Child Care Revenue . . . . . . . . . . . . . . . . . . . . . . . . . . . . . . . . $ _____

Minus Direct Costs . . . . . . . . . . . . . . . . . . . . . . . . . . . . . . − _____

Equals Gross Profit . . . . . . . . . . . . . . . . . . . . . . . . . . . . . . = _____

Gross Profit . . . . . . . . . . . . . . . . . . . . . . . . . . . . . . . . . . . . . $ _____

Minus Operating Costs . . . . . . . . . . . . . . . . . . . . . . . . . . . − _____

Equals Net Profit . . . . . . . . . . . . . . . . . . . . . . . . . . . . . . . . = _____

Net Profit . . . . . . . . . . . . . . . . . . . . . . . . . . . . . . . . . . . . . . $ _____

Minus Capital Expenditures . . . . . . . . . . . . . . . . . . . . . . . − _____

Minus Interest Expense . . . . . . . . . . . . . . . . . . . . . . . . . . . − _____

Minus Depreciation . . . . . . . . . . . . . . . . . . . . . . . . . . . . . − _____

Equals Income Before Taxes . . . . . . . . . . . . . . . . . . . . . . . = _____

Income Before Taxes . . . . . . . . . . . . . . . . . . . . . . . . . . . . . $ _____

Minus Income Tax Expenses . . . . . . . . . . . . . . . . . . . . . . . − _____

Equals Net Income . . . . . . . . . . . . . . . . . . . . . . . . . . . . . . = _____

# Balance Sheet

Statement of Assets and Liabilities as of _____, 20___

**Program Name:**

| ASSETS | | LIABILITIES | |
|---|---|---|---|
| **Current Assets** | | **Current Liabilities** | |
| Cash . . . . . . . . . . . . . . . . . . . | $ _____ | Accounts Payable . . . . . . . . | $ _____ |
| Accounts Receivable . . . . . . . | + _____ | Income Tax Payable . . . . . . | + _____ |
| Inventory . . . . . . . . . . . . . . | + _____ | Short-Term Loan Payable . . | + _____ |
| Prepaid Expenses . . . . . . . . | + _____ | Current Portion, Long-Term | + _____ |
| Total Current Assets . . . . . . | $ _____ | Total Current Liabilities . . . . | $ _____ |
| **Fixed Assets** | | **Long-Term Liabilities** | |
| Land, Building, Equipment, and Furniture . . . . . . . . . . . | $ _____ | Long-Term Loan Payable . . | $ _____ |
| Less Depreciation . . . . . . . . | − _____ | Other . . . . . . . . . . . . . . . . | + _____ |
| Total Fixed Assets . . . . . . . . | $ _____ | Total Long-Term Liabilities | $ _____ |
| **Total Current Assets** . . . . . | $ _____ | **Total Current Liabilities** | $ _____ |
| **Total Fixed Assets** . . . . . . | + _____ | **Total Long-Term Liabilities** | + _____ |
| **TOTAL ASSETS** . . . . . . . . | $ _____ | **TOTAL LIABILITIES** . . . . | $ _____ |
| | | **OWNER'S EQUITY** . . . . . . | $ _____ |
| TOTAL ASSETS . . . . . . . . . . | $ _____ = | TOTAL LIABILITIES + OWNER'S EQUITY . . . . . . . | $ _____ |

# APPENDIX

# C

# Library Resources

Benhan, Helen. (1992). *Parent Communication Tips From the Editors of Pre-K Today*. New York: Scholastic.

Child Care Directors. (1995). *250 Management Success Stories from Child Care Center Directors*. Redmond: Child Care Information Exchange.

Copeland, Tom. (1995). *The Basic Guide to Family Child Care Record Keeping* (5th ed.). St. Paul: Redleaf Press.

Copeland, Tom. (1997). *Family Child Care Contracts and Policies: How to Be Businesslike in a Caring Profession* (2nd ed.). St. Paul: Redleaf Press.

Copeland, Tom. (1999). *The 1999 Family Child Care Tax Workbook*. St. Paul: Redleaf Press.

Diffily, Deborah & Morrison, Kathy. (1996). *Family Friendly Communication for Early Childhood Programs*. Washington DC: National Association for the Education of Young Children.

Eiselen, Sherry. (1992). *The Human Side of Child Care Administration: A How-To Manual*. Washington DC: National Association for the Education of Young Children.

Fagella, Kathy & Horowitz, Janet. (1986). *Partners for Learning: Promoting Parent Involvement in School*. First Teacher Press.

Ferrar, Heidi M. (1996). *Places for Growing: How to Improve Your Child Care Center*. Princeton: Mathematica Policy Research, Inc., Rockefeller Foundation.

Ferrar, Heidi M. (1996). *Places for Growing: How to Improve Your Family Child Care Home*. Princeton: Mathematica Policy Research, Inc., Rockefeller Foundation.

Gestwicki, Carol. (1992). *Home, School and Community Relations: A Guide to Working with Parents*. Albany: Delmar Publishers.

Gonzalez-Mena, Janet. (1991). *Tips and Tidbits: A Book for Family Day Care Providers*. Washington DC: National Association for the Education of Young Children.

Hewitt, Deborah. (1995). *So This Is Normal, Too? Teachers and Parents Working Out Developmental Issues in Young Children*. St. Paul: Redleaf Press.

Kontos, Susan. (1992). *Family Day Care: Out of the Shadows and into the Limelight*. Washington DC: National Association for the Education of Young Children.

Montanari, Ellen Orton. (1992). *101 Ways to Build Enrollment in Your Early Childhood Program*. Phoenix: CPG Publishing Company.

Neugebauer, Bonnie & Roger. (1996). *On-Target Marketing: Promotion Strategies for Child Care Centers*. Redmond: Child Care Information Exchange.

Pruissen, Catherine M. (1998). *Start and Run a Profitable Home Day Care: Your Step-by-Step Business Plan*. North Vancouver: Self Counsel Press.

Sciarra, Dorothy June & Dorsey, Anne. (1999), *Developing and Administering a Child Care Center* (4th ed.). Albany: Delmar Publishers.

Soho Center & Redleaf Press. (1996). *The Business of Family Child Care with Tom Copeland: How to Be Successful in Your Caring Profession*. (Video). (Available from Redleaf National Institute, 450 N. Syndicate Avenue, Suite 5, St. Paul, MN 55104.)

Stonehouse, Anne. (1995). *How Does It Feel? Child Care from a Parent's Perspective*. Redmond: Child Care Information Exchange.

# Glossary of Terms

**Accounts Payable:**  Bills to be paid.

**Accounts Receivable:**  Money owed to the business.

**Assets:**  Value of everything owned by the business, including inventory, furniture, equipment, accounts receivable, cash, land, or property.

**Automobile Insurance:**  Additional insurance that may be required for business use of automobile. Providers who transport children as part of their child care service should review their policies.

**Balance Sheet:**  A document that shows *business assets* (what the business owns) and *business liabilities* (what the business owes) at a specific date. Also shows *owner's equity* (owner's personal investment plus profits).

**Beginning Cash:**  Total cash in checking account, savings, and petty cash fund at the beginning of any accounting period.

**Break-Even Analysis:**  A calculation of the level of sales necessary to pay all costs and reach profit goals.

**Cafeteria Plan:**  A benefit plan offered by businesses to employees, which allows employees to contribute a portion of their salary, tax-free, for the payment of dependent care expenses, out-of-pocket medical expenses, health insurance expenses, and/or retirement funds. Also known as a *flexible benefits plan*.

**Capital Expenditure:**  The amount spent for any asset or improvement that will be used in a business for more than one year.

**Cash Flow Projection:** An estimate of income and expenses for a specific period of time in the future (usually one year). Shows the pattern of money coming into and going out of the business, indicating how much, and when, cash will be needed for operation of the business.

**Checking Account:** A bank deposit against which checks can be drawn. Used to separate business income and expenses from personal income and expenses.

**Competitors:** A business or individual who provides a similar service. There are two types: *direct competitors* and *indirect competitors*. The direct competitors of a home-based child care business are other home-based child care businesses. The indirect competitors of a home-based child care business are all other types of child care available (centers, preschools, family members).

**Cost-of-Living Adjustment (COLA):** A change in salary or wage, based on the annual federal government's cost-of-living index. Many employers review the cost of living on an annual basis and adjust employee wages accordingly.

**Customer Profile:** A description of a typical customer. Categories often used to describe the customer include age, income level, education, profession, geographic area, lifestyle, or interests.

**Debt Service:** Money spent to repay debt, including both principle and interest.

**Deductions:** Business operation expenses that may be used to reduce business gross profit for tax purposes.

**Deficit:** A shortage in funds. Your checking account has a deficit when your balance is negative or "in the red."

**Depreciation:** Annual reduction in value of land, buildings, equipment, or furniture according to IRS schedule.

**Depreciation Schedule:** A table showing the amount per year and number of years over which an asset is depreciated.

**Direct Cost Percentage:** The percentage of child care provider's income that goes into business expenses directly related to caring for children.

**Direct Costs:** Expenses that vary with numbers of customers served. Also known as *variable costs*, or in other industries, *cost of goods sold (COGS)*.

**Ending Cash:** Total cash in checking account, savings, and petty cash fund at the end of any accounting period.

**Equity:** That portion of the total value of the business that is equal to the owner's investment plus profit.

**Equity Injection:** The value of items or money contributed by the owner for use by the business.

**Flexible Benefits Plan:** A benefit plan offered by businesses to employees that allows employees to contribute a portion of their salary, tax-free, for the payment of dependent care expenses, out-of-pocket medical expenses, health insurance expenses, and/or retirement funds. Also known as a *cafeteria plan*.

**Gross Profit:** Total revenue minus direct costs. Also known as *gross profit margin*.

**Gross Profit Percentage:** Gross profit divided by total revenue, times 100. The percentage of total revenue left after direct costs.

**Homeowners Insurance:** Additional coverage that may be required for business use of home. Providers who offer child care services in their homes should review their policies.

**Income Statement:** A document showing the sources and amount of income; the costs and expenses of providing service; and the amount of resulting profit (or loss) during a specific time period. Also known as a *profit and loss statement*.

**Income Tax Expense:** Annual or quarterly federal, state, and local taxes.

**Indirect Costs:** Expenses which do not vary with numbers of customers served. For a child care business, these include occupancy, utilities, telephone, training fees, printing. Also known as *fixed costs, operating costs,* or *overhead*.

**Interest Expense:** Interest paid on business loan or any other payable.

**Inventory:** Dollar value of consumable supplies and materials on hand.

**Labor Costs:** Include only the wages of caregivers, as part of direct costs.

**Liabilities:** Value of everything owed by the business, including accounts payable, income taxes, and loan payments. A *current liability* is a debt that will be payed within the current year; a *long-term liability* is a debt that will be carried for longer than the current year.

**Liability Insurance:** An insurance policy purchased by a child care business owner to protect him or her from being held liable for injuries, illnesses, deaths, or sexual molestation alleged to have resulted from child care.

**Ledger:** A record-keeping format that records business income and expenses by category.

**Loan Proceeds:**  The amount of money disbursed by a lender to a borrower.

**Major Equipment Expense:**  Funds spent for the purchase of equipment typically valued over $100 and used in the business for more than one year. These items can generally be depreciated.

**Market:**  The individuals or businesses most likely to purchase a product or service.

**Market Survey:**  Information gathered to reflect the numbers and preferences of potential buyers of a service.

**Marketing Strategy:**  A specific plan for attracting customers to a business.

**Net Income:**  Total income remaining after all expenses are paid.

**Net Profit:**  Total revenue minus direct costs and operating costs. Also known as *net profit margin.*

**Net Profit Percentage:**  Net profit divided by total revenue, times 100. The percentage of total revenue left after all expenses.

**Niche:**  A highly defined service tailored to a particular set of customers. Also known as *just what they are looking for!*

**Operating Costs:**  Expenses that do not vary with numbers of customers served. For a child care business, these include occupancy, utilities, telephone, training fees, printing. Also known as *fixed costs, indirect costs,* or *overhead.*

**Owner Draw:**  Money taken from profits of a business for the personal use of the owner.

**Price Fixing:**  The illegal activity of competitors agreeing to charge the same rates for products or services.

**Profitability:**  The ability of a business to make a profit, break even, or lose profit.

**Profit Goal:**  The amount of profit the owner expects the business to produce in a given time period.

**Projection:**  A calculation of future income and expenses.

**Receipt:**  A written statement acknowledging payment.

**Revenue:**  Income received by business.

**Surplus:**  An amount in excess of a certain number.

**Time/Space Percentage:**  A formula determining which portion of a home is used for business purposes and the financial value of that use. Used in calculating the percentage of a home child care provider's home expenses that can be deducted as business expenses for tax purposes.

# Index

Emergency medical information, 11
Employer-sponsored child care payment programs, 8
Ending cash, 61
Equity, 69
Equity injection, 62
Expenses, 22–23, 42
Expense worksheet, 33

Facility, and its appearance to outsiders, 86
Family rates, 26
Feedback, 52
Feeling words, 50
Filing system, 43, 47
Fixed expenses, 23
Flexible benefits plan, 8–9
Forms, reproducible, 119–132
Free advertising, 88
Full-time care, 25

Glossary of terms, 147–150
Goals, 1–2
Gross cost percentage, 60
Gross profit, 60
Guardians, and contracts, 6–7
Guilt, 17

Health relationships with families, 19
Holidays, 10
Hours of service, 7

Income, 42
Income statement, 63–65, 73, 135
Income tax expense, 66
Indirect competitors, 83
Indirect costs, 57
Innovator policies, 8
Inventory, 69

Labor costs, 57
Late pickup fee, 9
Leave days, 10
Ledger exercise, 44–46
Ledger systems, child care, 43
Liabilities, 69
Liability insurance, 55
Library resources, 145–146
Listening skills, 49–54
Loan proceeds, 61
Long-term liability, 69

Major equipment expense, 62
Market, knowledge of, 21–23

Marketing calendar, 83–85
Marketing strategies, 79–90
Market rate survey chart, 121
Market survey, 22–23
Maximum number of hours, 25
Minimum rate, 25

Net income, 66
Net profit, 61
Net profit percentage, 62
Niche, 24–25
Notice of contract changes, 13

Operating costs, 60

Operation expenses, 23
Overtime fee, 9
Owner draw, 62

Paid child absences, 25–26
Paraphrasing speaker's message, 50
Parents, and contracts, 6–7
Part-time care, 25
Passive aggressive communication style, 37–38
Passive communication style, 35–36
Payment schedule, 7–8, 27
Penalty fees, 9
Policy statement, 6, 103–112
Press release, 90
Price fixing, 22
Pricing concerns of parents, 30
Pricing objections, 30
Professional boundaries, 18
Professional image, 86
Profitability, 70
Profit and loss statement, 63
Profit goal, 23

Raises, 27
Rates, 7
Record-keeping system, 41–48
Records, retaining, 47
Release forms, 11
Renegotiating contract, 11
Reproducible forms, 119–132
Reservations, 7
Reserved care, 7, 25
Resource and referral service, 90
Resources, 145–146
Responding to speaker, 49–52
Responsibilities of provider, 91–92
Revenue, 57
Rights, of child care provider, 3–4